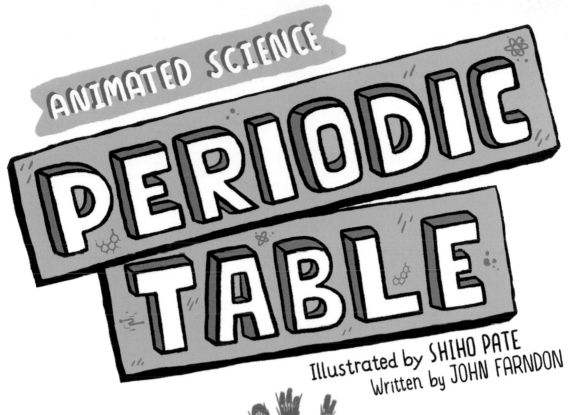

ANIMATED SCIENCE

PERIODIC TABLE

Illustrated by SHIHO PATE
Written by JOHN FARNDON

Scholastic Press • New York

CONTENTS

FIND YOUR FAVORITE ELEMENT

Blocks of elements react in similar ways. You can see which block an element is in by looking at its color in the periodic table on pages 6-7.

Alkali metals

Alkaline earth metals

Transition metals

Poor metals

Metalloids

Nonmetals

Halogens

Noble gases

Lanthanoids

Actinoids

HAVE YOU EVER WONDERED WHAT YOUR BODY IS MADE OF?

Or what a car is made of? Or the sea? Or the sky or the stars? Or the cat . . . ?
You might think it's all so complicated you could never know. Maybe it's millions
or billions of different things. Well, no, it's not! Amazingly, they're all made of ninety-
four naturally occurring substances called elements that get put together in billions of
ways. So with only these ninety-four elements, you can build everything in the universe.

About 150 years ago, a Russian scientist named Dmitri Mendeleev discovered that the elements can all be arranged in a special filing system called the periodic table. We're going to take you on a trip through Mr. Mendeleev's marvelous, magical table and beyond to meet each of the element characters. That's all of the ninety-four natural elements . . . plus twenty-four more that scientists have conjured into existence briefly in the laboratory.

Each element has its own special atom. What makes an element's atom so special is how many even tinier particles called protons it has in its core, or nucleus. So each element has its own identity tag, or atomic number, which is the number of protons that its atom has.

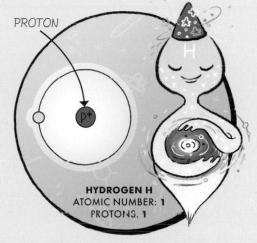

PROTON

HYDROGEN H
ATOMIC NUMBER: **1**
PROTONS: **1**

ELECTRON

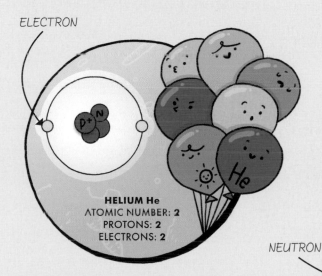

HELIUM He
ATOMIC NUMBER: **2**
PROTONS: **2**
ELECTRONS: **2**

An equal number of tiny particles called electrons whizz around the outside. These control how the atom reacts to others.

NEUTRON

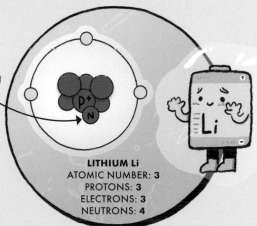

LITHIUM Li
ATOMIC NUMBER: **3**
PROTONS: **3**
ELECTRONS: **3**
NEUTRONS: **4**

There are also particles called neutrons in the nucleus, but we're not so interested in those.

THt PtRIUDIC TAbLt

THE MAP FOR OUR ADVENTURE WITH THE ELEMENTS

H	1

| HYDROGEN | |

So here we go! This is what to do. Start with the lightest atom of all, no. 1: hydrogen. Top left. Then zip across each row from left to right, one row at a time. At every single step, the atom gets a little heavier. At last you reach the heaviest of them all, no. 118: oganesson, bottom right.

The columns up and down are called GROUPS. Elements in each group tend to have similar characters.

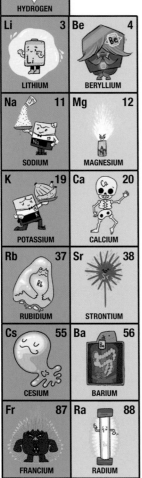

Li 3	Be 4
LITHIUM	BERYLLIUM
Na 11	Mg 12
SODIUM	MAGNESIUM
K 19	Ca 20
POTASSIUM	CALCIUM
Rb 37	Sr 38
RUBIDIUM	STRONTIUM
Cs 55	Ba 56
CESIUM	BARIUM
Fr 87	Ra 88
FRANCIUM	RADIUM

Sc 21	Ti 22	V 23	Cr 24	Mn 25	Fe 26	Co 2
SCANDIUM	TITANIUM	VANADIUM	CHROMIUM	MANGANESE	IRON	COBALT
Y 39	Zr 40	Nb 41	Mo 42	Tc 43	Ru 44	Rh 4
YTTRIUM	ZIRCONIUM	NIOBIUM	MOLYBDENUM	TECHNETIUM	RUTHENIUM	RHODIUM
La-Lu 57-71	Hf 72	Ta 73	W 74	Re 75	Os 76	Ir 7
LANTHANOIDS	HAFNIUM	TANTALUM	TUNGSTEN	RHENIUM	OSMIUM	IRIDIUM
Ac-Lr 89-103	Rf 104	Db 105	Sg 106	Bh 107	Hs 108	Mt 10
ACTINOIDS	RUTHERFORDIUM	DUBNIUM	SEABORGIUM	BOHRIUM	HASSIUM	MEITNERIUM

The rows across are called PERIODS, and atomic numbers go up as you travel from left to right.

La 57	Ce 58	Pr 59	Nd 60	Pm 61	Sm 6
LANTHANUM	CERIUM	PRASEODYMIUM	NEODYMIUM	PROMETHIUM	SAMARIUM
Ac 89	Th 90	Pa 91	U 92	Np 93	Pu
ACTINIUM	THORIUM	PROTACTINIUM	URANIUM	NEPTUNIUM	PLUTONIUM

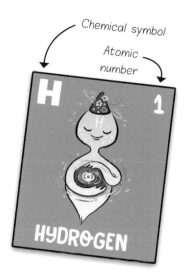

Chemical symbol

Atomic number

H 1

HYDROGEN

The box for each element is a collectible card with:
- An atomic number—the number of protons
- A chemical symbol—1, 2, or 3 letter identity code

The different colors show blocks of elements with quite similar characters. Find their names on page 3.

FIZZY AND GASSY
WELCOME TO GROUPS 1 AND 2. HANDLE WITH CARE!

WHO MELTS FIRST?

hydrogen

−434°F (−259°C)

potassium

146.3°F (63.5°C)

GROUP 1: THE FIZZIES

Wow, these guys are trouble! They're metals* on the extreme left edge of the table and they're the most reactive elements of all. Yes, they're so super-reactive that water makes them go off with a scary fizz and maybe a bang. That's why you don't often find them pure and alone—they're always joining with other elements.

* Hydrogen. Well, yes, six elements in the group are metals. That's why they're called the alkali metals. But the group also includes hydrogen, which is a gas and doesn't really fit. Awkward.

> GROUP 1:
> THEIR LONE OUTER ELECTRON IS EASILY LOST IN A REACTION!

Atomic Weight

1.00794

ALL GROUP 1 AND 2 ELEMENTS FORM ALKALINE SOLUTIONS (THE OPPOSITE OF ACID) WHEN THEY REACT WITH WATER.

GROUP 1:
ALKALI METALS

GROUP 2:
ALKALINE EARTH METALS

H 1		
HYDROGEN		
Li 3	Be 4	
6.941 LITHIUM	BERYLLIUM 9.012	
Na 11	Mg 12	
22.98977 SODIUM	MAGNESIUM 24.305	
K 19	Ca 20	
39.0983 POTASSIUM	CALCIUM 40.078	
Rb 37	Sr 38	
85.468 RUBIDIUM	STRONTIUM 87.62	
Cs 55	Ba 56	
132.905 CESIUM	BARIUM 137.327	
Fr 87	Ra 88	
FRANCIUM	RADIUM	

(Fr) 223

(Ra) 226

GROUP 2: THE GASSIES:

The Gassies are metals one column in from the Fizzies. They're not as super reactive, but don't underestimate them. When they touch water, they may not explode at once, but they make bubbles of hydrogen gas, and hydrogen gas can go off with a *bang*! And they're rarely found alone, either. They're called alkaline earth metals because they're often found mixed in earthy minerals.

> GROUP 2:
> TWO OUTER ELECTRONS CLING ON A LITTLE BETTER . . .

HYDROGEN

1
H
1.00794*

THE **LIGHTEST** AND MOST COMMON **ATOM** IN THE UNIVERSE BY FAR

IT'S WHAT KEEPS STARS BURNING

HYDROGEN IS A SUPER, SUPER LIGHT GAS—THE LIGHTEST, BY FAR!

A century ago, people filled balloons with hydrogen gas to float them up into the sky. But it's also super explosive, and after some nasty accidents, people switched to helium or hot air to fill balloons. Much safer! But if you want to build a nuclear bomb, hydrogen's explosiveness is useful. And it's what keeps the stars shining in the sky!

* On our element cards, you'll find the atomic weight here.

IT ALL STARTS HERE

Hydrogen was the very first atom—with just one lonely proton and one electron. That's why it's so incredibly light. It formed right at the beginning of the universe, and all the other elements were built from it later. Even now, 75 percent of the matter in the universe is hydrogen.

Stars are made mostly from hydrogen, too. Actually, stars shine mostly because their hydrogen burns fiercely in nonstop nuclear reactions. When the star's hydrogen finally burns out, the star collapses. That's when hydrogen atoms get crunched together to make other elements.

Still, hydrogen is amazing at forming teams. Hydrogen atoms love to get together with oxygen to make water. That's pretty vital for life. They also join up with carbon (and oxygen) in all kinds of ways to make pretty much all the solid materials life is made of, such as proteins.

Hydrogen fuel could make super-clean engines in the future. When hydrogen burns, it doesn't make nasty smoke; it makes pure water!

Our sun converts 600 million tons of hydrogen into helium every second! A tiny amount of the energy from that nuclear reaction comes to Earth as light and heat, powering all life's processes.

Did you know that **62** percent of the atoms in the **human body** are hydrogen?

HYDROGEN: At 68°F (20°C): Gas • Melting point: -434°F (-259°C) • Boiling point: -423°F (-253°C) • Color: None

LITHIUM IS A METAL. BUT IT'S SO LIGHT, IT ACTUALLY FLOATS ON WATER!

Really! It's so soft you can cut through it with a butter knife. And it's rather reactive—sprinkle water on it, and it creates bubbles of highly flammable hydrogen from the water. To stop lithium reacting even with damp air, you have to smear petroleum jelly all over it! And if you heat lithium, it will burn bright red, then burst into a brilliant light as it combines with oxygen in the air.

SUPER CHARGER

Lithium is old! Really old! It was one of the three kinds of atoms there with hydrogen and helium at the start of the universe. It has just three protons, and normally just three electrons to match, too.

Super simple, right? But one of those three electrons is alone on an outer ring. It's this lonely electron that makes lithium rather likely to react, as it tries to team up with other elements. It also helps make lithium great at storing electricity! The battery in your phone or computer relies on a special supercharged kind of lithium, called a lithium ion.

The problem is that lithium is now quite rare. In fact, it's never found alone naturally on Earth. It's locked into rare rocks, in places like Western Australia and Chile, and to get it, you have to mine the rocks and melt it out.

Lithium atoms that have lost their outer electrons are positively charged ions.

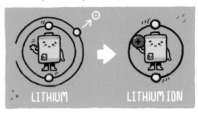

LITHIUM → LITHIUM ION

When you plug in your charger, crowds of lithium ions get pumped to one end of the battery. When you turn your phone on, the ions race back to the other end!

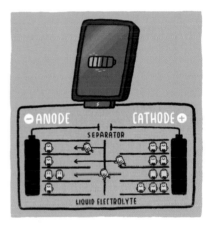

⊖ ANODE   CATHODE ⊕
SEPARATOR
LIQUID ELECTROLYTE

Lithium is so light it floats. So I've made a lithium raft.

SHINY!

That's a very strong reaction!

YIKES!

LITHIUM: At 68°F (20°C): Solid • Melting point: 358°F (181°C) • Boiling point: 2,448°F (1,342°C) • Color: Silvery white

SODIUM AND POTASSIUM

Na

K

WATER MAKES THEM GO BANG AND *FLASH*

SODIUM IS A FIRECRACKER OF A METAL. It's so light that it floats—but drop a grain in water and it melts, whizzes over the water, fizzes orange, then goes *bang!** It's also so soft you can cut it with a knife. Potassium's a firecracker metal, too. Like sodium, it floats. Drop a grain in water and it melts, whizzes over the water, fizzes lilac, then pops! A bigger ball sinks and makes so much hydrogen you get a huge explosion!*

*Don't EVER try this—it's extremely dangerous.

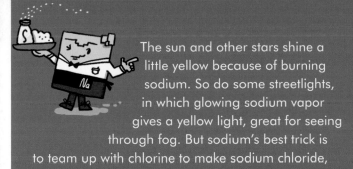

The sun and other stars shine a little yellow because of burning sodium. So do some streetlights, in which glowing sodium vapor gives a yellow light, great for seeing through fog. But sodium's best trick is to team up with chlorine to make sodium chloride, which is better known as salt!

Pure sodium's rare in nature, but it's widespread in salt. There's 50 million billion tons of salt dissolved in the oceans! There's also salt in our bodies. It plays a key role in the chemistry of cells, and animals like us can't survive long without it.

SODIUM: At 68°F (20°C): Solid
Melting point: 208°F (98°C)
Boiling point: 1,621°F (883°C)
Color: Silvery white

About a quarter of a billion tons of salt are produced each year from under the ground. Hot water is pumped down to dissolve underground salt, so it can be pumped up to the surface. Then the water is steamed off to leave the salt.

FOR YOUR TIRED POST-SPORTS BODY... ♥ LOVE. K

Like sodium, pure potassium is rare in nature, but there's a lot of it around, and life couldn't happen without it. It's an important fertilizer, helping plants grow. And it's vital in the body. Like sodium, it plays a central role in the chemistry of cells. Sodium sits mostly outside cells, with potassium inside, and the body can't survive unless that balance is right.

Actually, when a scorpion stings, it injects potassium salts into its victim, to paralyze and maybe kill it. Fortunately, for larger animals, like human beings, this is mostly just very painful. Ouch!

POTASSIUM: At 68°F (20°C): Solid
Melting point: 146.3°F (63.5°C)
Boiling point: 1,398°F (759°C)
Color: Silvery white

Potassium is found in many foods, but the best-known source is bananas.

4
Be
9.012182

BERYLLIUM

SUPERLIGHT AND SUPERTOUGH METAL FOR SPACESHIPS

GEMSTONES FOR GIANTS

BERYLLIUM IS ALMOST THE LIGHTEST METAL OF ALL.

Only lithium is lighter, and lithium's a bit of a softy. Beryllium is super tough. Strong. Doesn't corrode. And only melts at very high temperatures. So it would be great for spaceships. Oh, and it makes beautiful gems such as emerald and aquamarine. Only problem is—it's super rare . . .

WHAT A GEM

Beryllium's neighbors hydrogen, helium, and lithium were made right at the beginning of the universe. But oddly, beryllium came super late to the party. In fact, it was only created when giant stars exploded in supernova. That's why it's so rare. There may be some stars that have lots of it, but you won't find much on Earth!

In the ground, it's found in the minerals beryl and bertrandite. Beryl forms amazing gems that come in just about any color. There are dazzling green emeralds, deep-blue aquamarine, pink morganite, and yellow heliodor. What's more, it can grow crystals as big as tree trunks! A single crystal of beryl found in Malakialina, Madagascar was 59 feet (18 m) long, more than 11 feet (3.4 m) across, and weighed 419 tons (380 tonnes). That'd make some ring!

An emerald belonging to the famous American Rockefeller family was sold in 2017 for $5,511,500!

Beryllium is so tough, it bounces back neutrons. That's why it's used in nuclear warheads to intensify the explosion.

I want to paint my bedroom the beryl-color.

PAINT SHOP

BERYLLIUM: At 68°F (20°C): Solid • Melting point: 2,349°F (1,287°C) • Boiling point: 4,474°F (2,468°C) • Color: Silvery white

MAGNESIUM

12
Mg
24.305

FIERCE WHITE

BURNS

LIKE A FIREWORK

Mg

MAGNESIUM'S AN ABSOLUTE FIZZER, burning with a brilliant-white light like our sun! It's not so easy to set alight, especially when it's a solid metal. But grind it into powder or stretch it into ribbons—and *wooph!* Once it's burning there's just no stopping it. Magnesium's amazing at making connections with other elements, too, and it's in combinations that you'll mostly come across it.

WHITE LIGHT

Magnesium may be a metal, but living things really, really need it. It's what makes leaves green, for a start, because it's a key part of chlorophyll. And it's chlorophyll that turns leaves into solar powerhouses, taking energy from the sun to make plants grow. Without magnesium, leaves turn yellow and plants die.

Human bodies need magnesium just as much. It's vital for enzymes, the chemical messengers that keep the body working as it should. And it's vital for healthy bones. If your body's low on magnesium, eat nuts, dark chocolate, and leafy greens!

But it's best known for making a flash! In the old days, photographers used a flash of magnesium powder to give a brilliant light for portraits. And you'll find it lighting up the night in fireworks and sparklers!

Engineers add magnesium to aluminum to make extra-strong and light metal cars, airplanes, and even laptops.

Powdered magnesium makes brilliant fireworks, burning vivid, intense white. You can add metal salts to give colors, such as barium chloride for green, strontium chloride for red, and sodium salts for yellow.

In the old days, photographers used magnesium flashes to light pictures.

SAY CHEESE!

MAGNESIUM: At 68°F (20°C): Solid • Melting point: 1,202°F (650°C) • Boiling point: 1,994°F (1,090°C) • Color: Silvery white

Ca

40.078

CALCIUM

BONES WOULD BE **JELLY** WITHOUT IT

Ca

LIFE CAN'T DO WITHOUT IT

BY ITSELF, CALCIUM'S A SOFT, GRAY METAL, but link it up with a few other elements, such as carbon, and it turns white and tough as rock. In fact, it's so tough, you can build your bones from it, and shellfish make their shells from it. Bones, teeth, shells, skyscrapers— if you want a tough framework, you can count on calcium!

YOU'VE BEEN FRAMED

You've got two pounds of calcium in your body! But you don't clank as it's mostly in the form of calcium phosphate, and that's what the hard parts of your bones are made of. It's white and powdery, but super tough.

Shellfish make their shells from calcium carbonate. In fact, through Earth's long history, countless old shellfish shells piled up on the seabed and in time turned into vast rockbeds of calcium compounds. They're called limestones. Chalk is white and softer, and almost pure calcium carbonate.

Limestone is carved into blocks for building. It's also crushed to powder and mixed with sand, water, and gravel to make mortar, cement, and concrete. The Egyptian pyramids were stuck together by sticky lime cement, and there are no skyscrapers without concrete!

Pour vinegar on something made from calcium carbonate and watch it fizz! Wear safety goggles and avoid splashes!

In the 1820s, Thomas Drummond worked out that burning lime (calcium oxide) made a brilliant light. Actors loved the limelight!

They say I'm made of steel!

Huh, that's nothing. I've got pounds of calcium in my body!

CALCIUM: At 68°F (20°C): Solid • Melting point: 1,548°F (842°C) • Boiling point: 2,703°F (1,484°C) • Color: Silvery gray

37 Rb 85.468

RUBIDIUM

Rubidium would melt in your hand—but don't touch! It explodes if it comes into contact with water. And if not kept under a layer of grease, it bursts into flames! It spurts out radiation so regularly—at exactly 6,834,682,610.904324 times a second—that it's used as a counter for atomic clocks, the world's most accurate.

RUBIDIUM: At 68°F (20°C): Solid
Melting point: 102°F (39°C)
Boiling point: 1,270°F (688°C)
Color: Silvery white

Cesium is rubidium's gold-tinged twin, used for atomic clocks, too. Like rubidium, it reacts fiercely and violently with water and needs to be coated in grease to stop it from catching fire. And you only need a warm day to make it melt . . .

CESIUM

55 Cs 132.90545

CESIUM: At 68°F (20°C): Solid
Melting point: 83°F (28°C)
Boiling point: 1,240°F (671°C)
Color: Silvery gold

38 Sr 87.62

STRONTIUM

Strontium's a real live wire! When it meets water, there's an eruption of gas. When it meets air, it turns yellow and may burst into flame. And while natural strontium is quiet, its strontium-90 version is dangerously radioactive. Strontium salts make brilliant red fireworks, and paints containing strontium aluminate glow in the dark. Amazingly, a tiny bit in toothpaste helps reduce tooth pain.

STRONTIUM: At 68°F (20°C): Solid
Melting point: 1,431°F (777°C)
Boiling point: 2,520°F (1,382°C)
Color: Silvery gray

BARIUM

56

Ba

137.327

Barium's reactive when alone, and can glow in the dark. But mostly it teams up with other elements to make superdense powders such as barium sulphate, or barium "meal." In hospitals, patients with stomach illnesses may swallow this so that the meal sits in the stomach and gut, and shows up on scanners.

BARIUM: At 68°F (20°C): Solid
Melting point: 1,341°F (727°C)
Boiling point: 3,353°F (1,845°C)
Color: Silvery gray

FRANCIUM

87

Fr

223

Francium is super radioactive. That means its atoms are continually shooting out rays of particles and it breaks up! A heavy bombardment of these rays can be seriously dangerous. Francium forms when actinium splits like this. But francium itself lasts only twenty-two minutes before it starts to break up, scattering rays. That's why it's the world's rarest metal.

FRANCIUM: At 68°F (20°C): Solid
Melting point: 81°F (27°C)
Boiling point: 1,256°F (680°C)
Color: Unknown

RADIUM

88

Ra

226

Radium was the second-known radioactive element, discovered by Polish French chemist Marie Curie when she saw it glowing in the dark in her lab. People once thought radium was a miracle cure for ailments and a fun toy for kids. Now we know that radium's radioactivity makes it highly dangerous!

RADIUM: At 68°F (20°C): Solid
Melting point: 1,292°F (700°C)
Boiling point: 3,159°F (1,737°C)
Color: White

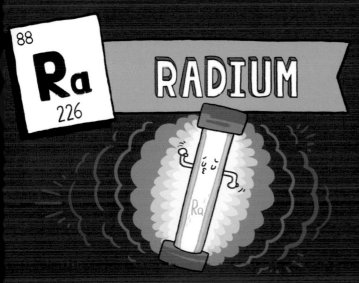

ALL ABOUT ATOMS

Atoms are minute, fuzzy clouds of energy. At their center, there's a core, or nucleus, of tightly packed particles called protons and neutrons. Spinning and whizzing round this is a cloud of super-tiny electrons.

Every time a proton is added to an atom, it makes a new element. An electron is usually added, too. Electrons are arranged in rings, or shells. The new electron is mostly added to the outer shell or the second shell. You can only fit certain number of electrons in each shell, though. Once a shell is filled, a new shell is created.

Atoms are held together by electricity. Electrons have a negative charge and protons have a positive charge. Opposite charges attract. So protons just about cling on to the electrons, even though the electrons would happily whizz off. Neutrons have no charge.

IONS AND ISOTOPES

Atoms usually have the same number of neutrons and electrons. But not always. Atoms that lose or gain electrons are called ions. Atoms that lose or gain neutrons are called isotopes.

SODIUM ATOM → LOSES OUTER ELECTRON → SODIUM ION

When a sodium atom loses its outer electron, it turns into a positively charged sodium ion, since it's now got more protons than electrons. It's called a sodium ion and it's labeled Na+.

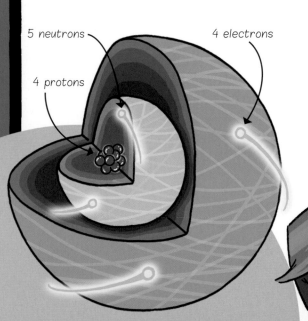

5 neutrons

4 electrons

4 protons

99.9 percent of the mass of an atom is in its nucleus. This is a beryllium atom.

In a solid, atoms are bonded together in a framework.

In a liquid, atoms vibrate loosely so they flow into any shape.

In a gas, they zoom around in all directions so the gas can shrink or expand into any space.

Most elements are normally solids. Only a few are gases. And just two, mercury and bromine, are liquids. But heat, chill, or squeeze them enough and they'll change their state. A melting point is when a solid gets so hot it becomes liquid. The boiling point is the hottest a liquid can get before becoming all gas.

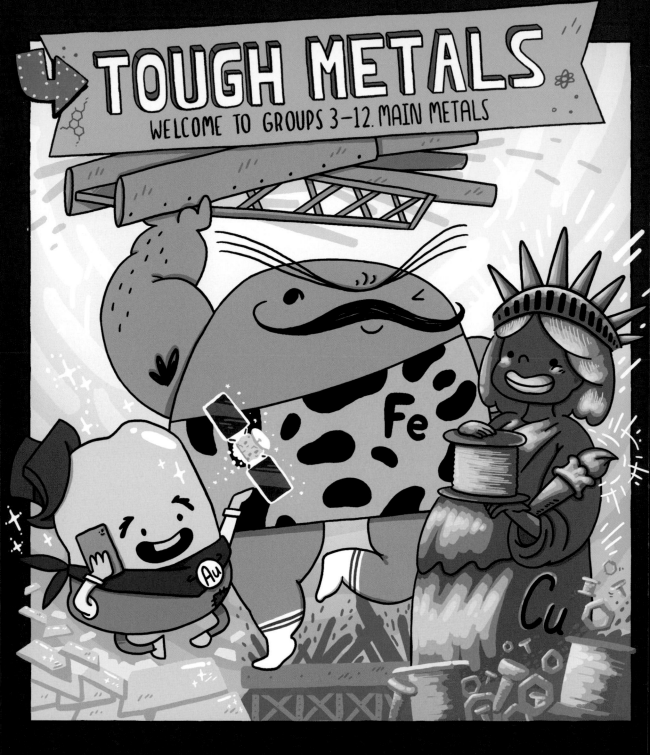

TOUGH METALS
WELCOME TO GROUPS 3–12. MAIN METALS

Fe

Au

Cu

WHO MELTS FIRST?

 mercury
-38°F (-39°C)

 silver
1,763°F (962°C)

 gold
1,947.5°F (1,064°C)

 copper
1,984°F (1,084°C)

TRANSITION METALS

When you talk about metal elements, these are the real deal. Iron, copper, gold, platinum, titanium, zinc . . . They're all here and they're all hard* and mostly shiny. Well, some of them do lose their shine if left in the air too long. And iron, of course, becomes rusty! But mostly this group is stable, and conducts heat and electricity well.

* MERCURY Well, yes, mercury is liquid, so not hard at all. But you only have to cool it enough and it becomes hard just like tin.

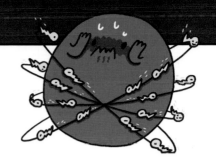

With Fizzies and Gassies, electrons are always added to the outer shell as you go from one element to the next. With transition metals, the transition *is how you can add up to thirty-two electrons to the second shell as you go from one metal to the next.*

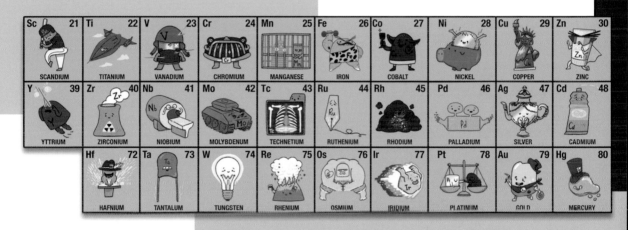

Sc 21	Ti 22	V 23	Cr 24	Mn 25	Fe 26	Co 27	Ni 28	Cu 29	Zn 30
SCANDIUM	TITANIUM	VANADIUM	CHROMIUM	MANGANESE	IRON	COBALT	NICKEL	COPPER	ZINC
Y 39	Zr 40	Nb 41	Mo 42	Tc 43	Ru 44	Rh 45	Pd 46	Ag 47	Cd 48
YTTRIUM	ZIRCONIUM	NIOBIUM	MOLYBDENUM	TECHNETIUM	RUTHENIUM	RHODIUM	PALLADIUM	SILVER	CADMIUM
Hf 72	Ta 73	W 74	Re 75	Os 76	Ir 77	Pt 78	Au 79	Hg 80	
HAFNIUM	TANTALUM	TUNGSTEN	RHENIUM	OSMIUM	IRIDIUM	PLATINUM	GOLD	MERCURY	

When they dissolve in water, compounds of transition metals show a range of bright colors.

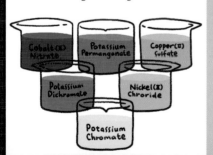

WHAT MAKES A METAL?

Metals are usually hard and shiny. That's because metals are crystals with atoms packed together in a neat and strong framework called lattice. In fact, the lattice is so strong, the atoms' electrons are free to drift around. It's these free electrons that make metals so good at conducting electricity—since the current passes on from electron to electron in a relay race. They're also why metals are shiny, because light bounces off them.

iron

2,800°F (1,538°C)

platinum

3,215°F (1,768°C)

chromium

3,465°F (1,907°C)

tungsten

6,192°F (3,422°C)

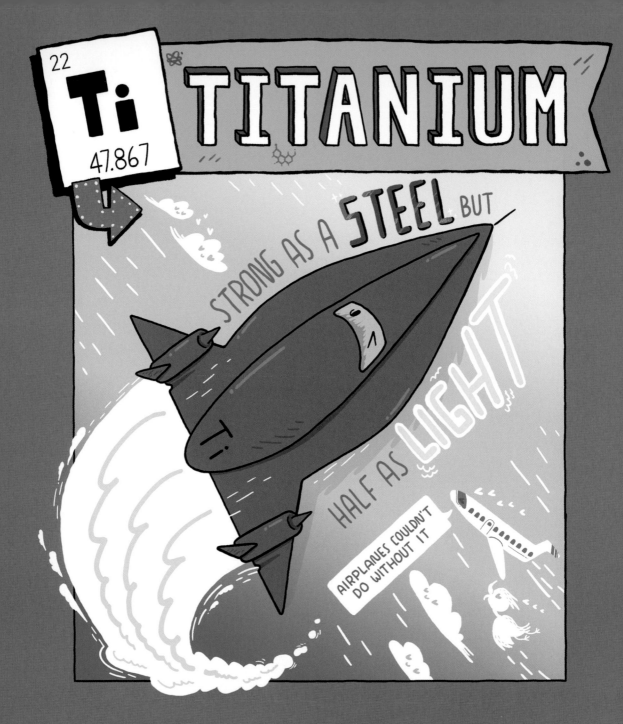

TITANIUM IS ONE OF THE STARS OF THE METAL WORLD.

It's tough as steel but half the weight. It doesn't get frail with age. And it's amazingly resistant to corrosion. Light, strong, good-looking. It's hard to resist. No wonder it has so many uses, from state-of-the-art jetplanes to lipstick!

TIGHT'N'LIGHT

Titanium has a big name! The Titans were the giant children of the gods in the myths of ancient Greece. But that's not what German scientist Martin Klaproth was thinking when he discovered titanium in 1795. He gave it the name because he thought it was a nice word. Little did he know how giant a metal titanium would become!

Titanium is so light and strong and resistant to corrosion that it's perfect for making airplanes and spacecraft. It's good for making top-of-the-line tennis rackets and racing bikes, too. It's not cheap, because it's not so easy to extract from the rocks in which it's found. But when money's no object, titanium's pretty hard to beat.

It's not toxic, either, so doctors love titanium because it's great for replacement hip joints or pins for holding broken bones together!

If you want dazzlingly white paint or paper, add a dash of titanium dioxide powder. Coat windows with titanium dioxide, and they clean themselves! Perfect for skyscrapers.

Shaped like a dagger, the Lockheed SR-71 Blackbird of the 1970s was the ultimate spy plane. It was 93 percent titanium and the fastest jet plane ever, reaching 2,193.2 miles per hour (3,529.6 kph).

TITANIUM: At 68°F (20°C): Solid • Melting point: 3,034°F (1,668°C) • Boiling point: 5,949°F (3,287°C) • Color: Silver

SCANDIUM

21
Sc
44.955912

Scandium is like a light, extra-tough aluminum. But there's not much around, so a little is added to aluminum to make a supertough alloy. Russian MiG fighter jets use it. So do great baseball bats. Traces of scandium are put in mercury-vapor streetlights to give a less harsh light. Mendeleev guessed that scandium existed because there was a gap in his table. Sure enough, ten years later, Swedish chemist Lars Nilson discovered it.

SCANDIUM: At 68°F (20°C): Solid
Melting point: 2,806°F (1,541°C)
Boiling point: 5,137°F (2,836°C)
Color: Silvery white

VANADIUM

23
V
50.9415

Superlight, supertough vanadium totally changed the world! Added to steel, it enabled Henry Ford to make the world's first mass-produced car, the Model T, from 1913. The same metal was used as armor against bullets during World War I. Today, if you need tough metal, vanadium steel is what you need. Like scandium, vanadium first came to the world's attention in Scandinavia, when Swedish chemist Nils Sefström identified it in the 1830s.

VANADIUM: At 68°F (20°C): Solid
Melting point: 3,470°F (1,910°C)
Boiling point: 6,165°F (3,407°C)
Color: Silvery gray

Cr CHROMIUM

24
Cr
51.9961

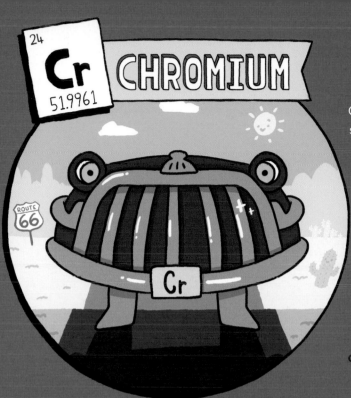

Chromium is the ultimate bling metal. Super shiny and tough, a chrome coating added dazzling glamor to the bumpers and grills of expensive American cars such as Chevrolets and Cadillacs in the 1950s. Chromium gives emeralds and rubies their color, and chromium compounds were used to give American school buses their characteristic yellow color in the past. Then people realized that chromium is toxic, so nowadays the yellow comes from cadmium.

CHROMIUM: At 68°F (20°C): Solid
Melting point: 3,465°F (1,907°C)
Boiling point: 4,840°F (2,671°C)
Color: Silvery gray

Mn MANGANESE

25
Mn
54.938049

Manganese is a hard but brittle metal. For thousands of years, it's been used as a powder in glassmaking to trap iron compounds and keep the glass clear. Knobs of manganese the size of potatoes are scattered across the ocean floor. They grow bit by bit as the metal settles on a grain of sand. Industrialists once thought they might be able to scoop up this free metal, but sea creatures are thankful they haven't managed it. Add manganese to steel prison bars . . . no prisoner can escape!

MANGANESE: At 68°F (20°C): Solid
Melting point: 2,275°F (1,246°C)
Boiling point: 3,742°F (2,061°C)
Color: Silvery gray

Fe

26

55.845

IRON

THE **MOST IMPORTANT** METAL IN THE WORLD

Fe

WITHOUT IRON, YOUR WHOLE WORLD WOULD **COLLAPSE.**

IRON RULES! OUR EARTH IS 35 PERCENT IRON, and it's the strong guy of the metal world. With traces of carbon and other metals added, dark-gray iron becomes super-tough, shiny steel. No wonder it's the most widely used metal in the world, forged into everything from kitchen sinks to supertankers. Even our bodies depend on it, using iron molecules to ferry oxygen around in the blood.

IRON IN SPACE!

Most of Earth's iron is far, far below us, forming our planet's dense, hot core, along with a little nickel. It sank there long ago when the newborn Earth was still a fiery, molten ball. Fortunately, there's still some left in the crust in iron-rich rocks called ores, and that's where we get it from.

All the world's iron was forged in stars long ago. In giant stars, there comes a time when the hydrogen and helium atoms that have fueled its glow are all burned out. The star collapses, smashing the atoms together to form new elements. Iron is the very last element that begins to form as it explodes as a "supernova". Iron and other elements hurled out by supernovae eventually formed the Earth.

Earth's CRUST is around 5 percent iron.

The MANTLE is rich in iron and magnesium.

The OUTER CORE is liquid iron and nickel.

The INNER CORE is solid iron and nickel.

Earth's MAGNETIC FIELD is generated by the movement of liquid iron in the outer core.

IRON: At 68°F (20°C): Solid • Melting point: 2,800°F (1,538°C) • Boiling point: 5,182°F (2,861°C) • Color: Silvery gray

COBALT

27
Co
58.9332

Cobalt is one of the four elements with magnetic powers. It gets its name from the German word for *goblin*. That's because medieval German miners kept digging up what they thought was silver—only to find it was cobalt! Cobalt chloride keeps up the cobalt brand of trickery as invisible ink. Nowadays, cobalt helps make superalloys that can take extreme temperatures in jet engines.

COBALT: At 68°F (20°C): Solid
Melting point: 2,723°F (1,495°C)
Boiling point: 5,301°F (2,927°C)
Color: Metallic gray

NICKEL

28
Ni
58.6934

Like cobalt, nickel is one of the magnetic foursome, along with iron and gadolinium. And like cobalt, medieval German miners had trouble with nickel, too! This time, they were tricked into thinking it was copper, so they called it "copper devil." Nickel's devilishly resistant to heat. Teamed with aluminum, it makes an alloy perfect for rockets and jets. Most people know nickel from the 5 cent coin, which is 75 percent copper and 25 percent nickel!

NICKEL: At 68°F (20°C): Solid
Melting point: 2,651°F (1,455°C)
Boiling point: 5,275°F (2,913°C)
Color: Silvery white

ZINC

30
Zn
65.409

Your body depends on zinc. If you don't have enough zinc in your food, you won't grow properly. You can get it by eating maple syrup, cheese, and oysters for a start! Zinc is a great blocker. Add it to sunscreen and it blocks harmful sun rays, though people stopped using zinc sunblock since it's so white you look like a ghost! Coat steel with zinc, and it stops air and moisture, dramatically reducing corrosion.

ZINC: At 68°F (20°C): Solid
Melting point: 788°F (420°C)
Boiling point: 1,665°F (907°C)
Color: Bluish white

If you want blue, cobalt's what you need. Beautiful blue glass, colored by cobalt, was found in the tomb of the Egyptian pharaoh Tutankhamun, dating from more than 3,000 years ago. Cobalt's been used to make amazing blue colors ever since.

Cobalt glass beads

Nickel's the metal from space! Most of the nickel we use comes from meteorites that crashed into Earth. One of the biggest hit the Sudbury area in Canada 1,849 million years ago, and left behind over 200 million tons of nickel!

If you see a shiny, golden metal anywhere, the chances are it's not gold but brass. Brass is a mix of about one-third zinc and two-thirds copper. It's a super-useful metal and much cheaper and tougher than gold. But it needs a lot of polishing to stay shiny!

29 Cu 63.546

COPPER

THE ONLY *RED* METAL

YOU CAN'T MISTAKE COPPER. NO OTHER METAL IS RED.

Plus it's the only metal except for gold and silver with a color named after it.
Copper's tough, but easily beaten into shape, or malleable, and stretched, or
ductile to make wires. Ductile matters because copper is such a good conductor
of electricity. All the world's electricity systems rely on copper wires!

SUNRISE METAL

For hundreds of thousands of years, in the Stone Age, humans relied on sharpened stones to make tools. But about 7,000 years ago, we discovered how to use copper! And that was pretty much it for the Stone Age . . .

Copper tools were soon the thing. They looked fabulous, but they were just a little bit soft. Then people realized you could add tin to copper to make tough bronze. Bronze was amazing for making anything from swords to cooking pots. The Bronze Age began about 5,000 years ago and we've been a metal crowd ever since.

Bronze isn't used much nowadays—iron is much cheaper and easier to make and even stronger. But copper's making a comeback! Only silver conducts electricity as well, so our electrical wiring is made from copper.

Left in the air, copper can turn from brilliant red to bright green as it combines with oxygen. This is called verdigris. You can see it all over the Statue of Liberty, which is covered in copper only 3/32nds of an inch thick.

The blood of lobsters, snails, and spiders is actually blue, not red! That's because the blood cells that carry oxygen around their bodies use copper molecules to hold the oxygen.

COPPER: At 68°F (20°C): Solid • Melting point: 1,984°F (1,084°C) • Boiling point: 4,644°F (2,562°C) • Color: Reddish-orange

Y

39
Y
88.90585

YTTRIUM

You may not have heard of yttrium but it's twice as common as lead. Its odd name comes from the tiny village of Ytterby in Sweden, where it was discovered in 1787. It's the soft touch of this tough foursome and the easiest to melt. But it can be used to make laser beams that can slice through steel like butter. And its isotope yttrium-90 can make needles for spinal surgery more precise than the best surgical scalpels.

YTTRIUM: At 68°F (20°C): Solid
Melting point: 2,772°F (1,522°C)
Boiling point: 6,053°F (3,345°C)
Color: Silvery white

40
Zr
91.224

ZIRCONIUM

OK, it's not diamond, but zirconium can certainly look like it. It's almost as tough as diamond, too. Zirconium's a metal, but it forms gem crystals called zircon that shine like diamond—but are much cheaper. And if you want to control a nuclear reaction, you need zirconium. It's so tough, it withstands the highest temperatures and neutrons just bounce off it. No wonder it's used for lining nuclear reactors and nuclear submarines.

ZIRCONIUM: At 68°F (20°C): Solid
Melting point: 3,371°F (1,855°C)
Boiling point: 7,968°F (4,409°C)
Color: Silvery white

NIOBIUM

41 Nb 92.90638

Niobium is a little soft in its raw state, but mix it with other metals and it becomes super tough and heat resistant. That's why the nozzles of space rocket engines are made from niobium alloys. Meanwhile, niobium alloys with tin or titanium make superconducting magnetic coils for medical scanners. And because niobium, in air, quickly gets a coat of oxide, it doesn't corrode—so it's great for making non-allergic jewelry.

NIOBIUM: At 68°F (20°C): Solid
Melting point: 4,491°F (2,477°C)
Boiling point: 8,571°F (4,744°C)
Color: Silvery gray

MOLYBDENUM

42 Mo 95.94

Molybdenum may have a silly sounding name but it's a tough cookie. Added to steel, it makes "moly steel," one of the hardest of all metals; it can take a lot of heat, too. Today, moly steel is used in high-speed drill bits. But it was also used in World War I to build the toughest tanks when it was found that conventional steel couldn't take a direct hit from an enemy shell. Molybdenum is also vital for life—without it, animals and plants can't make the proteins they need.

MOLYBDENUM: At 68°F (20°C): Solid
Melting point: 4,753°F (2,623°C)
Boiling point: 8,382°F (4,639°C)
Color: Silvery gray

PROFESSOR MENDELEEV AND THE BIG TABLE

Back in 1869, Russian Dmitri Mendeleev was just an ordinary chemistry professor writing a boring old chemistry textbook. Then one day he had a stroke of absolute genius. As far as Dmitri knew, there were sixty chemical elements. *Why not arrange them in a table for the book*, Dmitri thought. So he wrote them down in weight order, from the lightest, hydrogen, to the heaviest, uranium. But that wasn't the genius bit . . .

The genius bit was splitting the list into groups of seven, then laying each group in a row, or period, one on top of the other. That's how he captured a remarkable hidden pattern in the elements. It turns out that the element in the same place in each row has similar properties. So all the elements at one end of the row, for instance, are very reactive metals, while those at the other are unreactive gases. Amazing.

We now know the table works because of the structure of their atoms, and the number of electrons in their outermost layer.

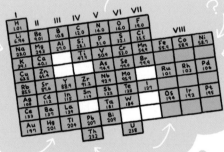

There were several gaps in Mendeleev's pattern. But that didn't bother him. He guessed there were unknown elements that would fill the gaps. And sure enough, over the next seventeen years, scientists discovered three missing elements—gallium, scandium, and germanium. Since then, more than fifty elements have been identified.

Tc 43 98 TECHNETIUM

Radioactive technetium breaks down and vanishes in a few million years! Amazingly, there's lots in red giant stars, where it's made. Now made by humans mainly in nuclear reactors, technetium is used in scanning for cancers.

TECHNETIUM: At 68°F (20°C): Solid
Melting point: 3,915°F (2,157°C)
Boiling point: 7,709°F (4,265°C)
Color: Silvery gray

Ru 44 101.07 RUTHENIUM

Ruthenium is very rare. But it's so resistant to corrosion that people really want it for electronics and solar cells. One fountain pen has a ruthenium tip so it never wears out.

RUTHENIUM: At 68°F (20°C): Solid
Melting point: 4,233°F (2,334°C)
Boiling point: 7,502°F (4,150°C)
Color: Silvery white

Rh 45 102.90550 RHODIUM

Super-shiny rhodium is 1,000 times rarer than gold. That's why Paul McCartney got a rhodium-plated disc in 1979 for being the bestselling music artist ever at that time. Most rhodium goes into catalytic converters, which make car exhausts less polluting.

RHODIUM: At 68°F (20°C): Solid
Melting point: 3,567°F (1,964°C)
Boiling point: 6,683°F (3,695°C)
Color: Silvery white

Pd 46 106.42 PALLADIUM

Like its cousins, rhodium and platinum, rare and shiny palladium is much in demand for catalytic converters. It's the lightest of the three, and great for corrosion-resistant electronic connections, which is why your smartphone probably has a little!

PALLADIUM: At 68°F (20°C): Solid
Melting point: 2,831°F (1,555°C)
Boiling point: 5,365°F (2,963°C)
Color: Silvery white

48 Cd — CADMIUM

112.411

Cadmium makes brilliant-yellow paints. The famous French painter Monet loved it. Unfortunately, we now know it's super toxic and poisonous, so its use in paints is being phased out. But it's still used in rechargeable NiCad (nickel and cadmium) batteries. Beware!

CADMIUM: At 68°F (20°C): Solid
Melting point: 610°F (321°C)
Boiling point: 1,413°F (767°C)
Color: Silvery white

72 Hf — HAFNIUM

178.49

Hafnium is often found with zirconium. But when it comes to nuclear power, they behave totally differently. Zirconium lets neutrons through. Hafnium stops them dead. So hafnium is used for the control rods that dampen down nuclear reactions, and zirconium is used to cover the fuel.

HAFNIUM: At 68°F (20°C): Solid
Melting point: 4,051°F (2,233°C)
Boiling point: 8,317°F (4,603°C)
Color: Silvery gray

73 Ta — TANTALUM

180.9479

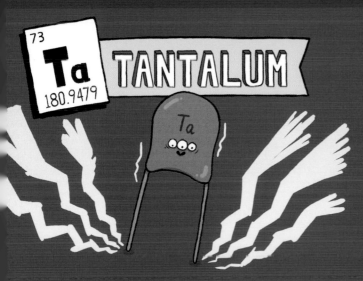

Tantalum is a soft, shiny metal used for coating electronic components in everything from video games to medical equipment. It's very rare and got its name because it seemed to tantalize the scientists who were searching for it in the early 1800s.

TANTALUM: At 68°F (20°C): Solid
Melting point: 5,463°F (3,017°C)
Boiling point: 9,856°F (5,458°C)
Color: Silvery gray

47
Ag
107.868

SILVER

SUPER SHINY MEDAL METAL

Ag

TOP CONDUCTOR FOR ELECTRICITY

GORGEOUS GOLD AND SHINY SILVER. The two top medal-winning metals. Silver's often the medal for coming second, but it's a winner when it comes to conducting electricity and heat. And it's super ductile (stretchy), too. All that makes it even better than copper for electric wires. And it's the shiniest metal of all. If only it wasn't so rare and expensive . . .

44

PRECIOUS METAL

You can actually find pure silver in the ground . . . if you strike lucky. You can find grains, wiry growths, and nuggets. But what you really want is bands in the rock called lodes. The Grosh brothers found a stupendous lode In Nevada back in 1857 worth $300 million. But both brothers died soon after, so the lode was named the Comstock Lode after their caretaker, Henry Comstock. Comstock had a difficult life and a bad end, too. Maybe not so lucky . . .

In the past, rich people wanted silver for swanky tableware and jewelry. But the servants had to clean it all the time, because silver goes black if exposed to the air. Nowadays, if you've got a smartphone, you've got a little silver. That's because it's an amazing conductor for the phone's tiny connections. Mind you, there's only about 0.00066 pounds . . .

Silver gave photography to the world! The first photographs were taken on plates covered with compounds of silver that darkened to record the picture when exposed to light.

Silver's chemical symbol, Ag, comes from *argentium*, the Latin name for silver. And *argentium* gave the whole country of Argentina its name, too, because there was a lot of silver there, once.

SILVER: At 68°F (20°C): Solid • Melting point: 1,763°F (962°C) • Boiling point: 3,924°F (2,162°C) • Color: Brilliant silver

74 W TUNGSTEN
183.84

No metal has a higher melting point or greater tensile strength—strength against pulling—than tungsten. It was once used for light bulbs as it glows white-hot without melting when electricity passes through it. Added to steel, it makes strong armor-plating for battle gear. Tungsten's symbol is W because medieval German miners called it "wolf dirt"; it got in the way when they were trying to melt tin out of rock.

TUNGSTEN: At 68°F (20°C): Solid
Melting point: 6,192°F (3,422°C)
Boiling point: 10,031°F (5,555°C)
Color: Silvery white

75 Re RHENIUM
186.207

Rhenium's even tougher than tungsten, with a melting point almost as high. Super-rare, pure samples are found in volcanoes! Rhenium was one of the last stable elements to be discovered, back in 1925. They only found .035 ounces (1 gm) of it by processing 1,455 pounds (660 kg) of molybdenum! But if you want a superalloy that can cope with extreme conditions, add rhenium to iron-nickel metal. It's used on top jobs like turning the engines of jet fighters.

RHENIUM: At 68°F (20°C): Solid
Melting point: 5,767°F (3,186°C)
Boiling point: 10,105°F (5,596°C)
Color: Silvery white

OSMIUM

76	
Os	
190.23	

No metal is harder or heavier than osmium. Wow, is it hard and heavy! Tungsten looks feeble and light next to osmium. It's super shiny like platinum and palladium, too. But osmium is ultra rare, though no one would wear it as jewelry because it gives off horrible-smelling fumes of osmium tetroxide. In fact, it's one of the smelliest of all elements. Its name comes from *osme,* which is Ancient Greek for *stink* . . .

OSMIUM: At 68°F (20°C): Solid
Melting point: 5,491°F (3,033°C)
Boiling point: 9,054°F (5,012°C)
Color: Bluish gray

IRIDIUM

77	
Ir	
192.217	

Iridium seems indestructible: hard, shiny, and the most corrosion-resistant metal known. When Smithson Tennant discovered iridium in 1803, he found that acid turned it into a rainbow of colors. So he named it after Iris, the Greek goddess of rainbows. It's common in meteorites. In fact, the dinosaurs may have been killed off by a meteorite that hurtled into the Gulf of Mexico 66 million years ago. That impact left a thin layer of iridium-rich clay covering the world.

IRIDIUM: At 68°F (20°C): Solid
Melting point: 4,435°F (2,446°C)
Boiling point: 8,002°F (4,428°C)
Color: Silvery white

PLATINUM

78
Pt
195.084

YOU'RE SUPER SHINY AND GLAMOROUS

GETS CHEMICAL REACTIONS GOING

PLATINUM IS THE MOST GLAMOROUS METAL ON THE PLANET.
It's super shiny and super rare. And unlike silver, it keeps its shine in air.
No wonder musicians who sell a million albums get a platinum disc—
it's better than a gold one! Platinum is also a terrific party starter or
catalyst—a chemical that gets other chemicals reacting together.

GETTING A REACTION

The people of Colombia in South America knew all about platinum thousands of years ago. But when the Spaniards arrived there 500 years ago, all they wanted was gold. It took centuries for them to realize that *platina del Pinto*, as they called it, was just as special, and perhaps even more so.

People like platinum for jewelry because it's super shiny and stays that way. But because it gets chemical reactions going, platinum is the secret ingredient in countless processes—oil refining, cleaning up car exhausts, making fiber optics, cancer drugs, computers, jet engines, and much, much more. It's only used in tiny amounts, but they're crucial. Platinum is good at staying unchanged. The original standard kilogram weight was made from platinum in 1799.

Platinum makes fumes belched out by cars a little cleaner. The fumes are filtered by catalytic converters. And the catalyst that does the converting is a thin coat of platinum on metal gauze.

The American Eagle is America's only platinum coin. It's supposed to be worth 100 dollars. But investors hold on to them and they can sell for thousands of dollars!

PLATINUM: At 68°F (20°C): Solid • Melting point: 3,215°F (1,768°C) • Boiling point: 6,917°F (3,825°C) • Color: Silvery white

79
Au
196.96655

GOLD

THE ONLY YELLOW METAL

STAYS SHINY FOREVER

GOLD IS THE ONLY YELLOW METAL ELEMENT AND IT'S RARE.
It never loses its shine because it doesn't corrode or mix much with other elements. That's why it's found in the ground in pure form. Gold was buried in the Earth billions of years ago, but comes out as shiny and golden as ever. Ancient treasures made from gold glitter like new.

ETERNAL SUNSHINE

The world's gold was forged long ago by exploding giant stars called supernova. It came here in meteorites, which crashed into Earth billions of years ago. It lies hidden in rocks, gleaming and perfect. It's hard to find, but it sometimes occurs in patches called lodes. In the past, when a lode was found, eager prospectors might flock to the site, as in California's 1848 Gold Rush.

About 190,000 metric tons have been dug up, and it nearly all still exists. It's a universally accepted form of payment. About a quarter of all gold ever mined is in bank vaults, like the Federal Reserve Bank of New York, in case paper currencies fail.

Today, most gold is used in jewelry. But it's also used more and more in smartphones and other electronic equipment, because it's a really good conductor of electricity and never corrodes.

The biggest gold nugget ever unearthed was the "Welcome Stranger" in 1869. It yielded 156.6 pounds (71 kg) of gold! Prospectors can "pan" for gold, swilling river water over sand in a special pan that separates out gold grains.

Gold is malleable, or easily shaped. One ounce can be hammered into an amazingly thin sheet 187 square feet (17 sq m) in size. This gold leaf can cover or gild surfaces so they shine.

What does a soccer player say when she signs a big contract?

GOOOOOLD!

GOLD: At 68°F (20°C): Solid • Melting point: 1,947.5°F (1,064°C) • Boiling point: 5,172.8°F (2,856°C) • Color: Metallic yellow

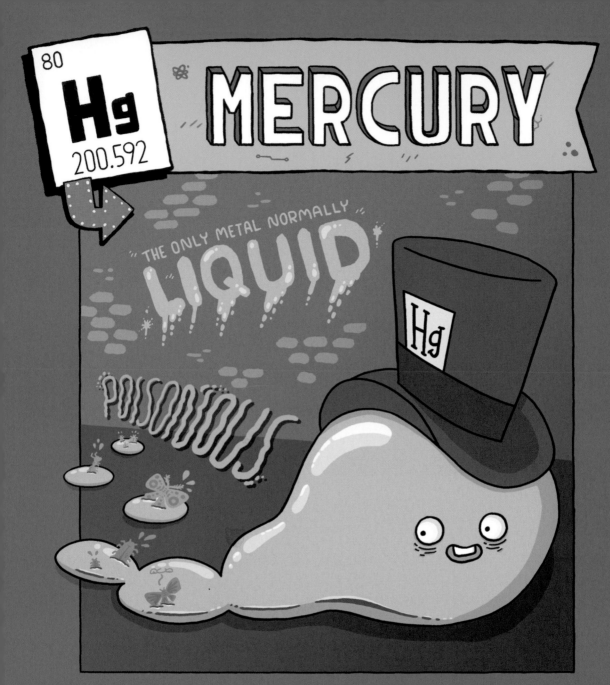

Hg

80

200.592

MERCURY

THE ONLY METAL NORMALLY LIQUID

POISONOUS

Hg

MERCURY IS THE ONLY METAL LIQUID AT ROOM TEMPERATURE.
In fact, it doesn't freeze solid until it gets very, very cold. But it's an entirely different liquid from water. It's about thirteen times denser. That means that if you tried walking on it you'd actually sink only to your ankles! But don't ever try it, even if you find enough mercury—it's seriously poisonous.

OOPS!

Hg

LIQUID METAL

For a long time, people thought mercury was magic. The Romans called it *hydrargyrum* in Latin, which means *liquid silver*. That's how mercury got its modern chemical symbol, Hg. In the Middle Ages, mercury was called *living* or *quicksilver*.

In fact, since ancient times, people thought mercury was so magical that they'd use it to treat illnesses. They didn't realize that mercury is in fact poisonous. English King Charles II died of mercury poisoning in 1685.

If you've read *Alice in Wonderland* by Lewis Carroll, you've met a character best known as the Mad Hatter. In Victorian times, hatters did indeed often go mad due to mercury poisoning. They dipped the felt for their hats in the metal to make the fibers mat together. Fortunately, we now know to steer clear of mercury, and it's critical that we dispose and recycle it safely.

Before people realized how dangerous it is, mercury was used for thermometers. It expands a lot even with the slightest temperature rise, so temperature changes show up very clearly. And it doesn't boil until it's 674.1°F (357°C), either.

Mercury mainly comes from the rock cinnabar that has a lovely red color. People once ground it into paint or face powder. But the mercury sulfide in cinnabar is poisonous!

What's so bad about MERCURY?

Nothing! I LOVE IT?

MERCURY: At 68°F (20°C): Liquid • Melting point: -38°F (-39°C) • Boiling point: 674.1°F (357°C) • Color: Silver

NEARLY METALS

WELCOME TO GROUPS 13–15. METAL OR NOT?

WHO MELTS FIRST?

 gallium  tin lead  aluminum

86°F (30°C)   449°F (232°C)   621°F (327°C)   1,220.58°F (660.32°C)

POOR METALS

These are also called "post-transition metals" and they're a bit grayer, duller, and softer than tough transition metals like iron. But that doesn't stop them from being very important and useful. They're great conductors of electricity and very easy to shape. Aluminum is the third-most abundant element in Earth's crust after oxygen and silicon, and very useful for drinks on the go!

Metalloids are quite hard and shiny but they're often brittle. That means they can crack like glass or chip like a mug when you hit them. They can even crumble to dust. That's why you usually alloy them with another metal if you want to make something strong.

We said use iron not a metalloid!

OH NO...

METALLOIDS

Metalloids are a kind of halfway house. They're a bit metal and a bit not metal. When it comes to conducting electricity, for example, some are semiconductors. That means sometimes they conduct electricity and sometimes they don't. Sound strange? But that's what makes them so great for electronics, because they act like switches. Boron, silicon, germanium, arsenic, antimony, tellurium, and polonium are all metalloids. Silicon plays a critical part in computers that have changed the modern world!

germanium

1,720°F (938°C)

silicon

2,577°F (1,114°C)

boron

3,769°F (2,076°C)

ALUMINUM

13
Al
26.982

DRAB SUPERSTAR

SUPER FRESH **AL**

SUPER LIGHT AND TOUGH

FROM SOFT DRINK CANS TO JET FIGHTERS

THERE'S MORE ALUMINUM ON EARTH THAN ANY OTHER METAL.
Yes, even iron! It looks a little drab but it's amazingly light and tough.
And aluminum doesn't corrode—it just gets a dark-gray coat of
aluminum oxide when exposed to the air. No wonder aluminum is
used for everything from saucepans to airplanes!

KEEPING IT LIGHT

The world is packed with aluminum but nobody knew it until 200 years ago. That's because it's hidden away in combinations with other substances, such as alum. For centuries, doctors used alum salts to stop bleeding and dyers used them to stop colors from running, but no one guessed they contained a metal. Then finally, in the early 1800s, scientists began to suspect alum's secret, and Danish scientist Hans Christian Orsted and German scientist Friedrich Wöhler made the breakthrough. Yes, there was a metal in alum that was named *aluminum*.

But aluminum was super rare and precious, until in the 1880s when it was discovered that you could get aluminum from aluminum minerals like bauxite by zapping them with electricity. Now aluminum is the world's most used metal after iron. It's so light and tough and resistant to corrosion that it's used for everything from soft drinks cans to power cables to bike frames. Early astronauts ate pureed food sucked through a straw from an aluminum tube!

YES WE CAN! Aluminum's the world's most recycled metal. Making new aluminum from bauxite uses a lot of electricity. It's much better to use it again! Recycle those cans!

Because it's so ductile—easily stretched—aluminum can be rolled into super thin sheets of shiny foil. Cooks wrap food in aluminum foil to seal in the juices when they're cooking.

OK boys, what went wrong with the robbery at the aluminum factory?

...

We were FOILED by security, boss!

ALUMINUM: At 60°F (20°C): Solid • Melting point: 1,220.58°F (660.32°C) • Boiling point: 4,470°F (2,470°C) • Color: Silvery white

THE METAL THAT MELTS LIKE BUTTER

WITHOUT IT, YOUR PHONE SCREEN MIGHT BE BLANK!

GALLIUM IS A BRIGHT, SHINY METAL. It may look quite tough, but it melts at just 86°F (30°C). Only mercury melts at a lower temperature. So if you made a spoon of gallium and tried to stir your hot drink, it would instantly vanish! Surprise! Indium squeaks faintly if you bend it. It's the crystals rejigging themselves. But that aside, it's a soft metal that's easy to shape. It's super rare and almost impossible to find by itself, but it thankfully can be found in zinc, tin, and lead ores.

SQUEAK!

Most metals transmit electricity well. Yet gallium does this only partly. Teamed up with metals such as arsenic, it's great for the semiconductors that all electronics rely on. If you've got a phone with an LED screen, or Blu-ray disc, for instance, you've got gallium! Doctors like it, too. There's a special version, or isotope of the gallium atom called gallium-67. This is a little radioactive, giving off rays. When injected into the body, it homes in on cancers. The tell-tale rays show cancer and are picked up by a scanner. This is called a gallium scan.

GALLIUM: At 68°F (20°C): Solid
Melting point: 86°F (30°C)
Boiling point: 3,999°F (2,203°C)
Silvery white

Neutrinos are tiny subatomic particles, almost impossible to detect. The sun sends out a continuous stream of them, which zoom through you without you noticing. Russian scientists filled a big bath with liquid gallium to trap a few neutrinos. It worked!

Hey you forgot your Oil Change!

Just like gallium, indium's a useful semiconductor for phones and computers. But its big selling point is that when teamed with oxygen in indium oxide, it sticks to glass, is transparent, and conducts electricity. That makes it perfect for sending the electric signals that give the picture on TVs, computers, and touchscreens. It's this purpose that most indium is used for. Indium, gallium, and tin are also used in combination in thermometers instead of toxic mercury. The only problem is that there's not that much indium left in the world . . .

Indium is super slippery. That's why racecar engineers coat ball bearings in indium instead of oil, which would slow things down.

INDIUM: At 68°F (20°C): Solid
Melting point: 314°F (157°C)
Boiling point: 3,762°F (2,072°C)
Color: Silvery gray

50 Sn 118.710 — TIN

Tin has a short name but a long history. Mix tin with copper and you get bronze, the first really tough metal humans ever used, from about 5,000 years ago. Tin cans have stored food for 200 years; a thin coat of the metal doesn't corrode. Nowadays, window glass for skyscrapers is made by floating molten glass on liquid tin.

TIN: At 68°F (20°C): Solid
Melting point: 449°F (232°C)
Boiling point: 4,715°F (2,602°C)
Color: Silvery white

81 Tl 204.3833 — THALLIUM

Thallium is a soft, heavy, radioactive metal that's been trouble right from the start! It was discovered in the 1860s from the green in its glow when it's heated. (Thallium comes from the Greek word for *green*). But two scientists, Sir William Crookes and Claude-Auguste Lamy, fought over who spotted it first. Crookes got the credit—which seems right since it's the metal of crooks!

THALLIUM: At 68°F (20°C): Solid
Melting point: 579°F (304°C)
Boiling point: 2,683°F (1,473°C)
Color: Silvery white

83 Bi 208.98040 — BISMUTH

It may look like thallium, but bismuth isn't nasty at all! It's very heavy, the heaviest metal of all that's not radioactive. Bismuth keeps us safe. Because it melts at quite low temperatures, it's used to make electric fuses. If there's a fault in your electric system, the bismuth melts and cuts off the circuit. Bismuth is used in fire alarms for exactly the same reason—setting off the alarm if it gets too hot.

BISMUTH: At 68°F (20°C): Solid
Melting point: 521°F (272°C)
Boiling point: 2,847°F (1,564°C)
Color: Silvery pink

In frosty weather, below 10°F (-12°C), tin turns to a powdery dust called "tin pest." That was a problem for old churches with organ pipes made of tin. It was also a problem for explorer Captain Scott, who stored kerosene fuel in tin cans for his trip to the South Pole in 1912. The fuel leaked in the cold and Scott and his crew did not survive for long without it.

Thallium is banned everywhere because it's super poisonous. The murderer in crime writer Agatha Christie's story *The Pale Horse* used it to sneakily kill off his victims. Thallium can be absorbed through skin, and once in the body, it pretends to be potassium and takes over all the vital body processes that use potassium. It's hard to detect and the victim dies slowly.

If you wear eye shadow or nail polish, bismuth is there to give it a pearly sheen. It's been used in cosmetics since ancient Egyptian times! You're more likely to think of bismuth as something that soothes your stomach, since it's the key ingredient in medicines like Pepto-Bismol.

LEAD

82
Pb
207.2

I . II . III

HEAVY
HEAVY

SECRET
POISONER

Pb

DRAB
SUPERSTAR

HEAVY!

LEAD IS ONE OF THE VERY HEAVIEST METALS,

as dull gray as a rain cloud, too. Few metals are as soft and easy to shape and bend. Lead's almost completely resistant to corrosion. And it melts at quite a low temperature. It's no wonder that until recently water pipes were made from lead, and people who fix them are plumbers, from lead's Latin name *plumbum*.

The lead in pencils is not lead at all; it's a kind of soft carbon called graphite!

HEAVY WEIGHT

The big problem with lead is that it's poisonous. In mild doses, it can give you stomach cramps and headaches. More prolonged exposure can damage the brain, giving you hallucinations and affecting intelligence. It's especially bad for children.

People in the past didn't only get lead poisoning from water pipes. Until recently, lead was added to gasoline to make it burn more smoothly—so everyone inhaled lead from exhaust fumes. Lead is now banned from water pipes, and so are lead additives in gasoline.

But lead's useful and there's still plenty around. Car batteries, for instance, rely on lead. Nuclear reactors are lined with lead to control the reactions because it's so dense. And X-ray rooms in hospitals are often lined with lead to protect staff and patients from radiation.

Queen Elizabeth I of England (1533–1603) used a mixture of lead and vinegar to cover up her smallpox scars. Some historians think that lead poisoning may have killed her!

The famous composer Beethoven and the painter Van Gogh may both have suffered from lead poisoning. Beethoven was given it by his doctor as a medicine. Van Gogh may have got it from paint; lead was used to make white color

LEAD: At 68°F (20°C): Solid • Melting point: 621°F (327°C) • Boiling point: 3,100°F (1,749°C) • Color: Gray

STAR MAKER

All the natural elements are children of the stars! Hydrogen, helium, and maybe lithium all formed very soon after the Big Bang event that scientists believe started the universe, nearly 14 billion years ago. The other elements were forged in the stars themselves, or when stars exploded or smashed together.

The Big Bang was an event of unimaginable energy. Hydrogen and helium formed in minutes as protons and neutrons smashed together. Scientists once thought lithium formed then, too. But they can't account for all the lithium around now. So they think most lithium formed later.

New stars are blazing powerhouses of hydrogen energy. They glow because gravity squeezes together the hydrogen atoms they are made of mega hard, triggering a nuclear reaction. The hydrogen atoms fuse together to make more helium. When you look at most stars, like our sun, you are seeing hydrogen making helium.

Eventually, after billions of years, there's too little hydrogen and helium to fuse. The dying star begins to collapse and atoms squeeze together to make bigger atoms and new elements. Pressure is most extreme at the star's core, so the new elements form like onion rings, with the smallest atoms on the outside and the biggest at the center.

Hydrogen

Helium

Carbon

Neon

Oxygen

Silicon

Iron

Nickel

Helium atoms join to form beryllium, and then carbon and oxygen.

Carbon atoms join to make sodium and neon.

Neon atoms join to make oxygen and magnesium.

Oxygen atoms join to make silicon.

Silicon atoms join to make iron and nickel.

Supernova: *Gallium* and *bromine* form.

Even the heart of a star can't fuse iron atoms. All atoms bigger than iron are forged at the end of a star's life. Some heavy elements are made when giant stars explode in a supernova. Others form when two super dense "neutron" stars smash together.

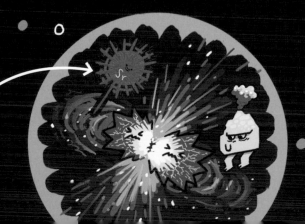

Smashing neutron stars: *gold, uranium,* and *strontium* form.

BORON AND SILICON

PLANTS WOULD DIE WITHOUT IT

BUILDS THE WORLD!

BORON AND SILICON ARE BOTH METALLOIDS, they're a bit like metals and a bit like nonmetals. They mostly appear as dull-brown powders but don't underestimate them! Boron may be rare but plants can't survive without it. And silicon, when joined with oxygen, makes tough crystals that build most of Earth's rock. In fact, there's silicon everywhere—in sand, in your computer and smartphone, in window glass, and in bottles!

People knew about white borax powder (sodium and boron) in ancient times. Goldsmiths of old used it to help shape gold. And if you wanted to get rid of mold or house pests, borax did the job. In fact, borax was so much in demand that a thousand years ago, camels carried it all the way along the old Silk Road from Tibet of China to Arabia and Europe. But no one knew it contained boron.

In 1732, French chemist Geoffroy the Younger burned borax and saw a strange green flame, and wondered if there was something in the powder. But it wasn't until 1909 that American scientist Ezekiel Weintraub isolated pure boron for the first time.

BORON: At 68°F (20°C) Solid
Melting point: 3,769°F (2,076°C)
Boiling point: 7,101 °F (3,927°C)
Color: Varied

Silicon and boron can both be mega hard. Boron carbide makes bulletproof vests and tank walls! But they can also mix to form stretchy, bouncy Silly Putty. The silicon is stretchy silicone—made from long molecules of silicon, oxygen, and other organic chemicals.

Silicon for chips needs to be mega pure. First, it's mined from secret sources of high-purity quartzite. Then it's refined in high-tech units called fabs to make rod-shaped crystals or "ingots" of 99.99999 percent pure silicon. The ingots are sliced by diamond tools into microscopic wafers to make chips.

Silicon is definitely not a loner. Whenever it gets the chance, silicon teams up with other elements. Its favorite partner is oxygen. Together, they make super-abundant minerals called silicates that make up 90 percent of Earth's crust as well as gems like amethyst, jade, and topaz. Your phone, and every other electronic device, depends on "chips", or tiny sheets, of silicon. Silicon is a semiconductor —that is, it can change its ability to conduct electricity, so it's perfect for the microscopic switches these devices need.

SILICON: At 68°F (20°C) Solid
Melting point: 2,577°F (1,414°C)
Boiling point: 5,909°F (3,265°C)
Color: Bluish, metallic

32 Ge 72.631

GERMANIUM

Silvery-white, brittle, rare, metalloid germanium was discovered in—you guessed it—Germany, in 1886 in a chunk of rock from a deep silver mine. It was the missing element between silicon and tin predicted by Mendeleev. It's one of the first semiconductors—materials whose ability to conduct electricity can be switched on and off. For a long while, silicon ruled the semiconductor roost. But germanium is coming back into fashion!

GERMANIUM: At 68°F (20°C): Solid
Melting point: 1,720°F (938°C)
Boiling point: 5,131°F (2,833°C)
Color: Silvery white

51 Sb 121.760

ANTIMONY

Antimony is a metalloid a bit like lead—and one of the few substances to expand when it becomes solid, like water does. Ancient Egyptians used to outline their eyes with a dramatic black line using powdered antimony sulfide. But antimony is also poisonous, and in the nineteenth century, many murderers used it to secretly kill. In the Middle Ages, people took antimony pills as a laxative—then "recovered it" to use again . . . Gross!

ANTIMONY: At 68°F (20°C): Solid
Melting point: 1,167°F (631°C)
Boiling point: 2,889°F (1,587°C)
Color: Silvery gray

TELLURIUM

52
Te
127.60

You may come across tellurium in DVDs and Blu-ray discs. It's a rare metalloid that usually forms as a dark-gray powder. The tellurium is coated onto the disc to help form the thin layer that carries the music and video data. But like antimony, tellurium's poisonous, and people who handle tellurium for a while get stinky "tellurium breath"— which smells like they've been eating far too much garlic! The solution is said to be eating lots of oranges and lemons!

TELLURIUM: At 68°F (20°C): Solid
Melting point: 842°F (450°C)
Boiling point: 1,810°F (988°C)
Color: Silvery white

POLONIUM

84
Po
209

Polonium is big trouble. It's so radioactive that its most common isotope actually glows in the air. It was discovered in 1898 by Marie and Pierre Curie in the uranium ore they were studying. They named polonium after Marie's native Poland. What they didn't bargain for was that it's super radioactive and poisonous, and probably helped kill Marie. The heat it creates was used to keep the lunar rovers Russia sent to the moon in the 1970s working.

POLONIUM: At 68°F (20°C): Solid
Melting point: 489°F (254°C)
Boiling point: 1,764°F (962°C)
Color: Silvery gray

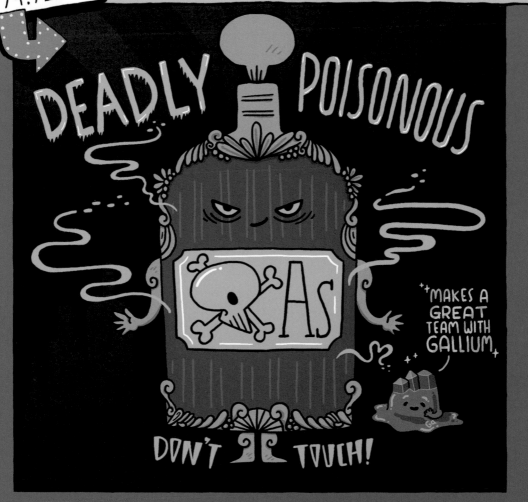

33

As

74.92160

ARSENIC

DEADLY POISONOUS

As

MAKES A GREAT TEAM WITH GALLIUM

DON'T TOUCH!

ARSENIC IS SHIFTY. It comes in various allotropes—different forms of the same element. Sometimes it's like a lump of old black coal. Sometimes it's a bright-yellow, waxy solid. Expose the yellow form to light and it turns into a brittle, metallic-gray form, that tarnishes in the air. Amazingly, arsenic doesn't normally melt but sublimes straight to gas. Its boiling point is lower than its melting point!

KILLER!

Arsenic is very poisonous, and so are many of its compounds. Too many people throughout history have been killed by it, and exposure to even small traces of it can make you very ill. No wonder there are strict laws about handling it.

After his defeat at the Battle of Waterloo in 1815, French Emperor Napoleon was sent to the remote island of St. Helena in the middle of the Atlantic. He died just six years later, and he may have been poisoned by his wallpaper! It was colored with the dye Paris green, which is made from arsenic.

Many terrible murderers have used arsenic, too. Just .0035 ounce (100 mg) of it kills, which is tough to trace in a body. But in 1836, a British chemist invented a sensitive test for detecting arsenic in murder victims.

If you see a ruby-red rock, beware—it could be realgar. And if you see a yellow amber rock, steer clear—it could be orpiment. Realgar and orpiment are minerals rich in arsenic.

It might be poisonous, but arsenic is useful, too. Teamed with gallium, it's good for "doping" electronic chips and making them run faster.

This room is too shabby for the Emperor of France!

I got you some nice new wallpaper!

ARSENIC: At 68°F (20°C): Solid • Melting point: 1,503°F (817°C) • Boiling point: 1,137°F (614°C) • Color: Gray

THE IN-BETWEENERS
WELCOME TO GROUPS 3 PLUS, THE GATECRASHERS

Scientists measure the lifetime of radioactive elements like the actinoids in terms of half-life—the time it takes for half of their atoms to break up.

La 57	Ce 58	Pr 59	Nd 60	Pm
LANTHANUM	CERIUM	PRASEODYMIUM	NEODYMIUM	PROMETHIUM
Ac 89	Th 90	Pa 91	U 92	Np
ACTINIUM	THORIUM	PROTACTINIUM	URANIUM	NEPTUNIUM

WHO LASTS LONGEST?

nobelium  lawrencium plutonium

58 minutes   10 hours   88 years

LANTHANOIDS

The 15 lanthanoids, along with yttrium and scandium, are often called Rare Earth Elements or REEs. But they're not really rare or earthy. They're silvery metals and they got the name because they're scattered widely in ores, in small amounts. They're all much the same chemically, but they vary a lot magnetically—and some like neodymium make superpowered magnets. You'll find them in hybrid cars, superconductors, and strong magnets.

ACTINOIDS

The 15 actinoids are big atoms. They're seriously dangerous because they're all highly radioactive—breaking down and sending out radioactive rays. Except for uranium and thorium, most have to be made artificially because in nature they just break down and vanish. But radioactivity makes uranium and plutonium useful for nuclear power, and terrible weapons.

Actinoids   Lanthanoids

Lanthanoids and actinoids are gatecrashers at the periodic table! The rest builds up neatly as an extra electron is added to the outside of an atom to make a new element. With these guys, the electron is added inside. They all have the same number of electrons outside, which puts them between at the bottom left of the table. So chemists have given them a side table of their own!

62	Eu 63	Gd 64	Tb 65	Dy 66	Ho 67	Er 68	Tm 69	Yb 70	Lu 71
SAMARIUM	EUROPIUM	GADOLINIUM	TERBIUM	DYSPROSIUM	HOLMIUM	ERBIUM	THULIUM	YTTERBIUM	LUTETIUM
94	Am 95	Cm 96	Bk 97	Cf 98	Es 99	Fm 100	Md 101	No 102	Lr 103
PLUTONIUM	AMERICIUM	CURIUM	BERKELIUM	CALIFORNIUM	EINSTEINIUM	FERMIUM	MENDELEVIUM	NOBELIUM	LAWRENCIUM

curium

uranium

thorium

15.6 million years   700 million years   14 billion years

57 La LANTHANUM
138.90547

Lanthanum's a metal so soft, you can cut it with a knife. But its big claim to fame is being the first of the lanthanoid elements—once known as rare earth metals, because they were, wrongly, thought rare. Lanthanum's never found alone. It's occurs only in two minerals, monazite and bastnaesite. It helps make batteries for hybrid cars, and is amazingly good at clearing algae from ponds.

LANTHANUM: At 68°F (20°C): Solid
Melting point: 1,688°F (920°C)
Boiling point: 6,267°F (3,464°C)
Color: Silvery white

58 Ce CERIUM
140.116

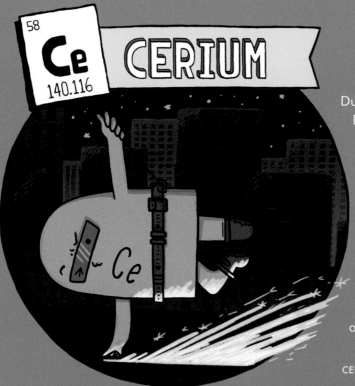

Dull-gray cerium looks a little like iron. But scrape it with a knife and you get a shower of sparks! Expose splinters of cerium to air and it bursts into flames—very useful for film special effects! No wonder some firelighters are made with cerium. Self-cleaning ovens are coated with it because it turns greasy fumes into easy-to-wipe ash. It's also useful for cleaning up messes such as car exhaust fumes and diesel engines, and helps in nontoxic paints.

CERIUM: At 68°F (20°C): Solid
Melting point: 1,463°F (795°C)
Boiling point: 6,229°F (3,443°C)
Color: Iron gray

PRASEODYMIUM

59 **Pr** 140.90765

Praseodymium got its weird name, which means *twin green*, because it goes green from the oxygen in air. Scientists love praseodymium, because in experiments it helps them slow the speed of light nearly to a standstill. Its odd way of getting colder when exposed to a changing magnetic field also helped scientists create the coldest temperature ever: -459.65°F (-273.144°C). *Brrr!*

PRASEODYMIUM: At 68°F (20°C): Solid
Melting point: 1,715°F (935°C)
Boiling point: 6,368°F (3,520°C)
Color: Silvery gray

NEODYMIUM

60 **Nd** 144.242

Soft, silvery neodymium's the magnet king! It can be joined with iron and boron to make NIB magnets that lift 1,000 times their own weight. Tiny NIB magnets make earbud earphones and computer hard drives work. And they're great in light, electric motors for model aircraft and electric cars. Neodymium also helps make some of the best, most intense laser beams, called Nd:YAG lasers because they're powered by Nd (neodymium) and YAG (yttrium, aluminum, and garnet).

NEODYMIUM: At 68°F (20°C): Solid
Melting point: 1,870°F (1,021°C)
Boiling point: 5,565°F (3,074°C)
Color: Silvery white

61 Pm 145

PROMETHIUM

Promethium is super rare! That's because it's radioactive, so it breaks up amazingly quickly. This is very unusual for a small atom. But it's why promethium wasn't discovered until 1945—and it wasn't until 1963 that scientists managed to isolate more than .02 pounds (10 g). But there's a longer-lasting variety that makes blue paint and helps in tiny "atomic batteries," no bigger than a pea, that last for five years. It's perfect for heart pacemakers, guided missiles, and miniature radios.

PROMETHIUM: At 68°F (20°C): Solid
Melting point: 1,908°F (1,042°C)
Boiling point: 5,432°F (3,000°C)
Color: Silver

62 Sm 150.36

SAMARIUM

Some of the first personal headphones relied on powerful samarium-cobalt mini-magnets. Now these magnets have been superseded by even better NIB magnets but they're still used in microwaves, because they stay magnetic even at high temperatures. One compound of samarium, samarium sulfide, makes black crystals that are great semiconductors for electronics. But if you scratch them, they turn gold and they become fully conducting!

SAMARIUM: At 68°F (20°C): Solid
Melting point: 1,962°F (1,072°C)
Boiling point: 3,261°F (1,794°C)
Color: Silvery white

EUROPIUM

63 Eu 151.964

Europium helps catch forgers! Genuine euro banknotes have a trace of europium in a metallic strip. Under UV light, the europium glows red. Fakes notes don't glow, so banknotes can be checked automatically for forgery. And if your low-energy light bulbs have a nice warm glow, rather than a harsh white one, that's due to europium, too. Europium is great at absorbing neutrons, making it useful for control rods in nuclear reactors.

EUROPIUM: At 68°F (20°C): Solid
Melting point: 1,519°F (826°C)
Boiling point: 2,784°F (1,529°C)
Color: Silvery white

GADOLINIUM

64 Gd 157.25

Europium may be great at absorbing neutrons for nuclear reactors, but gadolinium's even better. Gadolinium's pretty much the best. It's also very magnetic, but only when it's cool. Warm it above 66°F (19°C) and it loses its magnetic powers. If you go the hospital for an MRI (magnetic resonance imaging) scan, they sometimes inject a dose of gadolinium that spreads through your body and shows up on the scan to highlight problems.

GADOLINIUM: At 68°F (20°C): Solid
Melting point: 2,394°F (1,312°C)
Boiling point: 5,923°F (3,273°C)
Color: Silver

Tb

158.92535

TERBIUM

Terbium glows green. Weird! It can also make your table speak or your window sing! That's because terbium alloys have a special quality—they get shorter or longer in a magnetic field. A terbium alloy called Terfenol-D can be made into a rod that stretches or shrinks in response to an audio signal. If placed just touching a surface, the rod makes the surface vibrate like a loudspeaker. This alloy can also help make sonar instruments that bounce sound waves to detect things underwater.

TERBIUM: At 68°F (20°C): Solid
Melting point: 2,473°F (1,356°C)
Boiling point: 5,846°F (3,230°C)
Color: Silvery white

66

Dy

162.5

DYSPROSIUM

Dysprosium means *hard to get.* That's because the French scientist who discovered it in 1886 had to work really hard to separate it out. It's so reactive that it just doesn't exist by itself naturally. It's not only soft enough to cut with a knife, it corrodes quickly in air and dissolves in acid. And if you put it anywhere near water, it makes hydrogen and explodes! All the same, it's a tiny but key ingredient in NIB magnets and used in electric cars. But supplies are low.

DYSPROSIUM: At 68°F (20°C): Solid
Melting point: 2,565°F (1,407°C)
Boiling point: 4,644°F (2,562°C)
Color: Silvery white

67 Ho HOLMIUM
164.93032

Holmium's the doctor's friend. It's not magnetic itself, but it can concentrate the power of magnets dramatically. This is really important when a superstrong magnet is needed—such as in hospital MRI (magnetic resonance imaging) scans. It's great for eye surgery, too, since it's added in traces to a YAG (yttrium, aluminum, garnet) laser to make a super accurate laser beam for surgery. Unfortunately, it's quite rare.

HOLMIUM: At 68°F (20°C): Solid
Melting point: 2,662°F (1,461°C)
Boiling point: 4,928°F (2,720°C)
Color: Silvery white

68 Er ERBIUM
167.259

Erbium makes glass pink. If you ever want rose-tinted spectacles, erbium's the key. Like europium, it can be added to low-energy light bulbs to give them a warmer glow. If you ever have laser surgery at the dentist, erbium may be powering the beam. It gets its name from the village of Ytterby in Sweden, which has three other elements named after it—terbium, yttrium and ytterbium—which were all first identified there.

ERBIUM: At 68°F (20°C): Solid
Melting point: 2,784°F (1,529°C)
Boiling point: 5,194 °F (2,868°C)
Color: silver

THULIUM

Most lanthanides have something special about them that makes them useful. Not poor thulium. It's a rare soft metal found mostly in the mineral monazite. But it does have some interesting qualities. You can cut it with a knife and it catches fire at a temperature lower than paper. It's used in lamps for stage lighting. And it's named after Thule, the ancient name for Scandinavia.

THULIUM: At 68°F (20°C): Solid
Melting point: 2,813°F (1,545°C)
Boiling point: 3,542°F (1,950°C)
Color: Silver gray

69
Tm
168.93421

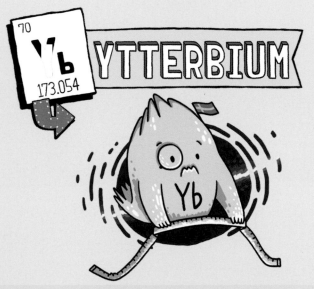

YTTERBIUM

Ytterbium's not as rare as once thought—not since quite a lot was found in China. It's a bit odd when conducting electricity. Normally, it conducts electricity. But if you squeeze it really hard, it becomes a semiconductor. The more you squeeze, the less it conducts. That makes it great for pressure gauges in extreme conditions such as nuclear explosions!

YTTERBIUM: At 68°F (20°C): Solid
Melting point: 1,506°F (819°C)
Boiling point: 2,185°F (1,196°C)
Color: Silver

70
Yb
173.054

LUTETIUM

Lutetium was once the world's most expensive element. It would cost you seventy-five dollars for a thirtieth of an ounce! It's cheaper now they've found better ways of extracting it, but it's still expensive. It's the hardest and densest of all the lanthanides—and lanthanides have unusually densely packed atoms. It's named after the Latin word for Paris. It was discovered there in 1907.

LUTETIUM: At 68°F (20°C): Solid
Melting point: 3,006°F (1,652°C)
Boiling point: 6,156°F (3,402°C)
Color: Silver

71
Lu
174.9668

Lighting engineers like thulium. Coat a light bulb with thulium, and it catches the glow of the light and re-emits a fantastic emerald green. Thulium also makes lasers that are good for very precise surgery. And if you want a personal radiation dose detector, thulium's what you need.

The most useful form of ytterbium is not natural at all. Called Yb-169, it emits gamma rays. That makes it great for giving the radiation in portable, emergency X-ray devices, where there's no power source for a full-scale machine.

In 2001, lutetium showed geologists that the Earth's crust is 200 million years older than they thought. A kind of lutetium called Lu-176 breaks up slowly into hafnium at a very precise rate. Measuring the amount of hafnium in rocks showed that the crust is seriously ancient—4.3 billion years old!

TEAMING UP

Atoms and elements are rarely alone for long! Many team up or react with each other to form new substances. A formula is a symbol for all the atoms in a team, with little numbers showing how many atoms of each there are.

Two atoms of the same element can bond together to make a molecule. Oxygen is found naturally as molecules of two atoms.

$$O_2$$

Compounds get made when atoms of two or more different elements combine. The atoms are always in the same ratio. So in carbon dioxide, there is always one carbon atom for every two oxygen atoms.

$$CO_2$$

Compounds have a life of their own, very different from the atoms that made them.

Mixtures are when elements come together without their atoms joining at all! Air is a mix of elements, such as oxygen and nitrogen, and compounds, such as carbon dioxide.

In a chemical reaction, such as a fire burning or iron rusting, chemicals meet and react to each other. The molecules may break apart and their atoms get swapped around. This creates new compounds or releases elements.

Combustion is a chemical reaction that makes fire! For example, hydrocarbons react with oxygen to make heat and light, water, and carbon dioxide. You can find hydrocarbons in wood.

Baking powder contains the compound sodium bicarbonate. It's made from sodium, hydrogen, carbon, and oxygen. Its formula is $NaHCO_3$. Add the powder to a cake mix and when you pop it in the oven, the compound reacts with acids in the powder. The reaction makes bubbles of carbon dioxide, making your cake light and airy!

89 Ac 227 ACTINIUM

You can't miss actinium in the dark—it makes the air around it glow bright blue! That's because it's super radioactive, about 150 times more radioactive than radium. The rays it gives off make the air glow by bumping its atoms and charging them with electricity. Even so, it can be used to treat cancers. And oceanographers follow the radioactive trace of tiny amounts of it deep in the ocean. This can reveal how changes in the climate are affecting how our oceans circulate.

ACTINIUM: At 68°F (20°C): Solid
Melting point: 1,922°F (1,050°C)
Boiling point: 5,788°F (3,198°C)
Color: Silver

90 Th 232.038 THORIUM

Named for the Norse god, Thor, thorium is super radioactive like uranium, and three times as abundant. Thorium's radioactivity is what keeps the inside of Earth hot, along with uranium. It may soon replace uranium as the fuel for nuclear power, and provide all the world's electricity for 1,000 years. In World War II, the Allies found a stockpile of thorium in Germany and thought the Germans were planning to build a nuclear bomb. In fact, they wanted to make thorium-flavored toothpaste, not knowing the danger!

THORIUM: At 68°F (20°C): Solid
Melting point: 3,182°F (1,750°C)
Boiling point: 8,650°F (4,788°C)
Color: Silver

91 Pa PROTACTINIUM
231.03588

Protactinium is one of the most radioactive of all elements. That's why people once thought they might make atomic bombs from it. But actually, it's far too rare and although traces of it exist in the green mineral tobernite, it's very tricky to extract. And anyway, why would you bother? Protactinium's radioactivity makes it one of the most toxic elements on the planet. Mind you, if you've got a smoke detector, you may have a trace of it in your house—too little to hurt—because the americium in it decays to make a little protactinium.

PROTACINIUM: At 68°F (20°C): Solid
Melting point: 2,854°F (1,568°C)
Boiling point: 7,280°F (4,027°C)
Color: Silver

93 Np NEPTUNIUM
237

Like protactinium, neptunium is super-radioactive and super rare. Even so, you might just have some in your house. Like protactinium, a little may form when the americium in smoke detectors breaks up. It's found in nature in partnership with uranium. But there's so little of it and it's so hard to extract that it wasn't until 1940 that it was finally identified. The scientists called it neptunium because it comes after uranium in the periodic table, just as the planet Neptune is next to Uranus in the solar system.

NEPTUNIUM: At 68°F (20°C): Solid
Melting point: 1,191°F (644°C)
Boiling point: 7,056°F (3,902°C)
Color: Silver

92
U
238.02891

URANIUM

BIG and SUPER DANGEROUS

OTHERS POWER BEHIND NUCLEAR BOMBS and POWER STATIONS

HEAVY!

URANIUM'S A REAL HEAVYWEIGHT. It's the biggest of all natural elements, and that makes it stand out. It's so big that it's continually radioactive—breaking down and sending out incredibly dangerous rays. It's a hard, silvery metal but it reacts with most nonmetal elements to form compounds. In air, it turns black with a thin coat of uranium oxide.

NUCLEAR DRIVER

There's an awesome power locked inside the giant nucleus of an atom of uranium. It took the immense power of a supernova giant star explosion to forge such big atoms, so they are jam-packed with energy.

In nature, uranium's energy is released gently as the nucleus gradually disintegrates, helping keep Earth hot inside. But atomic bombs smash the uranium nucleus in a fraction of a second—unleashing it in a sudden devastating blast. The splitting is called fission.

Nuclear power stations release the energy in a more controlled way to create the heat to make steam to drive electricity turbines. A uranium fuel pellet that's the size of your finger contains as much energy as 1 ton (.9 tonnes) of coal. Even so, the engineers have to put a lot of ingenuity into keeping it all safe.

A lichen named *Trapelia involuta* loves uranium! In 1998, it was found growing on spoil heaps from an old uranium mine in England, happily taking up the uranium.

The power of uranium was appallingly revealed when, during World War II, in 1945, the US Air Force dropped a nuclear bomb on the Japanese city of Hiroshima. The dreadful explosion destroyed the city in an instant and killed more than 80,000 people,

URANIUM: At 68°F (20°C): Solid • Melting point: 2,070 °F (1,132 °C) • Boiling point: 7,468 °F (4,131°C) • Color: Silvery gray

94
Pu
244

PLUTONIUM AND CURIUM

96
Cm
247

NUCLEAR POWERHOUSE

PLUTONIUM AND CURIUM ATOMS ARE EVEN BIGGER
and even more power-packed than Uranium. Whoa. Both are
dangerously radioactive. Curium is so radioactive it glows reddish
pink in the dark! But both are almost never found naturally.
Instead, they are made in nuclear reactors. Plutonium is made
by bombarding uranium with neutrons. Curium is made by
bombarding plutonium with neutrons.

Plutonium packs a terrifying amount of energy into its nucleus. The bomb dropped on Hiroshima, Japan, in 1945, contained 132 pounds (60 kg) of uranium. A second bomb, dropped on Nagasaki just a few days later, contained a tenth as much plutonium yet generated an even more powerful explosion. The damage these bombs did was appalling, and thankfully, no plutonium bomb has been dropped since.

Now plutonium is used in fast-breeder nuclear power stations. And robot spacecraft use it as a tiny but long-lasting power source for long voyages through the solar system.

PLUTONIUM: At 68°F (20°C): Solid
Melting point: 1,183°F (639°C)
Boiling point: 5,842°F (3,228°C)
Color: Silvery gray

When a young Queen Elizabeth II visited an atomic research institute in the 1950s, she was given a plastic bag full of plutonium! She noticed how warm it was. That's because it was radioactive! No harm was done.

US scientist Glenn Seaborg and his team discovered curium in 1944, but kept it top secret because it was wartime. When the war ended in 1945, Seaborg let his secret out on the kids' radio show Quiz Kids!

Curium isn't named because it's curious, but after the famous scientific duo Marie and Pierre Curie who discovered the first radioactive elements. Curium isn't as dangerous as plutonium. It makes the perfect, tiny power source for heart pacemakers. It can also be used on space probes to make a special machine to do an instant analysis of rocks on the moon and Mars. Some scientists suggest converting the world's ever-growing stockpile of plutonium into curium. Curium is not only much shorter lived, but can be used for more useful things than terrible bombs.

CURIUM: At 68° (20°C) Solid
Melting point: 2,453°F (1,345°C)
Boiling point: 5,600°F (3,100°C)
Color: Silvery gray

SUPER MIXERS
WELCOME TO GROUP 17 AND PARTS OF 14-16

WHO MELTS FIRST?

 fluorine

 nitrogen

 chlorine

C°

-364°F (-220°C)   -346°F (-210°C)   -151°F (-102

THE BIG SIX

This is the big six—well, the big five—carbon, nitrogen, oxygen, phosphorus, and sulfur, plus selenium. Oxygen, carbon, and nitrogen are the third-, fourth-, and seventh-most abundant elements in the universe. The air is made up almost entirely of nitrogen and oxygen. Your body is 65% oxygen, 18% carbon, and 3% nitrogen. And 10% is hydrogen, which is almost an honorary member of this group.

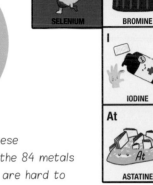

C 6 CARBON	N 7 NITROGEN	O 8 OXYGEN	F 9 FLUORINE
P 15 PHOSPHORUS	S 16 SULFUR	Cl 17 CHLORINE	
Se 34 SELENIUM	Br 35 BROMINE		
I 53 IODINE			
At 85 ASTATINE			

There are only a few of these nonmetals, compared with the 84 metals of the periodic table. They are hard to pin down—solids, liquids, and gases!

Join many of this lot with hydrogen (and maybe a little oxygen) and you get an acid. Pure sulfuric acid can destroy flesh and burn through solid metal. But with fluorine, chemists now turn acids into "superacids." Fluoroantimonic acid is a billion times more corrosive than sulfuric acid and will eat its way out of any container—except Teflon!

THE HALOGENS

The halogens are violently reactive and seriously smelly. They're the "-ines" such as fluorine and chlorine—the last group in the table but one. In pure form, they can be nasty. Fluorine will attack all kinds of things. Chlorine was used as poison gas in World War I. But get them in compounds, and they can be super useful. Partnered with sodium, chlorine makes plain old sea salt!

bromine
19°F (-2°C)

phosphorus
111°F (44°C)

sulfur
239°F (115°C)

6

C

12.0107

CARBON

FORMS TEN MILLION COMPOUNDS

ALL **LIFE** DEPENDS ON IT

CARBON FORMS MORE COMPOUNDS THAN ALL THE OTHER ELEMENTS PUT TOGETHER! In fact, there's a whole branch of chemistry, called organic chemistry, devoted entirely to carbon. It comes in very different forms, or allotropes—diamond, graphite, soot, and fullerene—which could hardly be more different. Diamond is one of the world's hardest solids and slippery graphite is one of the softest.

HARD

SOFT

THAT'S LIFE

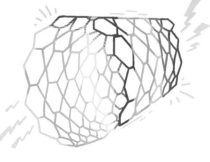

Without carbon, there would be no life at all. Carbon has an amazing ability to join with oxygen and hydrogen to form complicated molecules. It's these compounds that make all the materials of life, from the cellulose that makes all plants to the proteins in animals. In fact, most of the food you eat is made of carbon compounds.

People talk about their carbon footprint. That's because hydrocarbons are the main component of oil, coal, and gas. We dig them up and use them to power our lives. This releases carbon dioxide, which collects in the air and traps the sun's heat, causing damaging changes to the climate. Your carbon footprint is a measure of how much carbon dioxide you add to the air by, for instance, traveling by car and burning fuel.

Fullerenes come in sheets one-molecule thick, with carbon molecules linking in a mesh like chicken wire. They're usually rolled into balls called buckyballs or amazing microscopic tubes called nanotubes.

Diamonds are beautiful and just about the world's hardest natural substance which is great for cutting. Scientists have made Q-carbon, a synthetic diamond that is 60 percent harder than a natural one!

Hey, man ... what's your carbon footprint?

Literally, nothing.

CARBON: At 68°F (20°C): Solid • Melting point: 6,422°F (3,550°C) • Boiling point: 6,917°F (3,825°C) • Color: Silvery white

7

N
14.00674

NITROGEN

PLANTS CAN'T DO WITHOUT IT

MAKES THINGS GO "BANG!"

YOU MAY NOT KNOW IT, BUT RIGHT NOW YOU'RE BATHING IN NITROGEN!

About 78 percent of the air is nitrogen. Fortunately, it's colorless, odorless, and unreactive. You breathe it in and out all the time, but it has no effect on your body. Nitrogen compounds, though, are very different! Life, especially plants, depends on nitrogen compounds. And they're so reactive that some of the world's most powerful explosives are nitrogen compounds.

IT'S IN THE AIR

There's nitrogen everywhere! It's in the air, in the soil, under our feet, and in the water we drink. It plays a key role in life. The way that it cycles in multiple forms through living and nonliving things, in the oceans, on land, and in the air, is called the nitrogen cycle.

Without nitrogen from the soil, plants cannot grow properly. But it needs to be in the right balance. Too little and plants turn yellow and shrivel, but too much is toxic. Farmers add nitrogen-rich fertilizers to the soil to make crops grow better. Nitrogen is also vital for DNA, the biological molecules that give every living thing its instructions for life. Nitrogen helps form the rungs that hold the ladder of DNA together, and without it DNA would just fall apart.

At -320°F (-196°C), nitrogen becomes liquid. Put a banana in liquid nitrogen and it becomes so hard you can use it as a hammer! Liquid nitrogen also preserves organs such as the heart for transplants.

Nitrogen makes bangs! Teamed up with potassium, it makes saltpeter for gunpowder. With hydrogen, oxygen, and carbon, it makes highly explosive nitroglycerin. Another nitrogen compound, azide, explodes to inflate car air bags and save lives.

Hey did you see that?

That's just Ray in her nitrogen cycle.

THIS?!

NITROGEN: At 68°F (20°C): Gas • Melting point: -346°F (-210°C) • Boiling point: -320°F (-196°C) • Color: None

OXYGEN IS EARTH'S MOST ABUNDANT ELEMENT.
It's an invisible gas, about 20 percent of the air we breathe, and we can't live without it for more than a few minutes! Unlike nitrogen, which is about 78 percent of the air, oxygen is highly reactive. It makes fires burn. Metals rust, or "oxidize" as they react with it. The oceans are made from one of oxygen's compounds—water.

BREATHER

Amazingly, there was no oxygen at all in the air until about three billion years ago. But then, microbes in the oceans began to take energy from the sun by photosynthesis, like plant leaves. In return, they filled the air with oxygen and thanks to plants, it has stayed that way since.

Now animals, including us, can't live without it! When you breathe in, the lungs transfer oxygen from the air into the blood. The blood carries the oxygen to every cell to release energy from the food you eat. You exhale carbon dioxide. The higher you go on Earth, the fewer oxygen molecules there are, and in space, there are hardly any! That's why people get altitude sickness from climbing mountains, and astronauts extract oxygen from water!

Oxygen doesn't burn itself but it feeds fire! Burning is a combustion reaction: what happens when a substance reacts with oxygen from the air to create light and heat.

Most oxygen molecules have two oxygen atoms. But some, named ozone, have three. A thin layer in the atmosphere, rich in ozone, helps shield Earth against harmful UV rays from the sun. The ozone layer was damaged by pollution, though now it's recovering.

Hey, what's up?

I'm busy converting oxygen into carbon dioxide.

How's that?

BREATHING GIRL...

OXYGEN : At 68°F (20°C): Gas • Melting point: -362°F (-219°C) • Boiling point: -297°F (-183°C) • Color: None

RECIPE FOR A BODY

You may not know it, but you're a walking periodic table! The human body is a complicated chemical recipe, and to make one you need over 60 elements, each in just the right amount. That's more than two-thirds of all the natural elements.

Ninety-three percent of your body's mass is just three elements—oxygen, hydrogen, and carbon.

Over half the mass of your body is water and that's where you'll find a lot of the oxygen and hydrogen.

Oxygen, hydrogen, and carbon join in many combinations to make muscles, fats, and other, solid materials. In fact, you're basically those three elements with a scattering of other elements thrown in!

Besides the three biggies, your body also needs another eight vital elements—nitrogen, calcium, phosphorus, potassium, sulfur, sodium, chlorine, and magnesium.
And then there are many elements that are in the body in small traces—which is why they are called trace elements. The body needs tiny quantities of at least a dozen of these, including iron, iodine, and zinc, to stay healthy.

Your body also contains poisonous chemicals such as lead, cadmium, mercury, and arsenic. If they're in tiny quantities, your body can cope. But raised levels of any one of these can make you ill.

WHAT ARE YOU MADE OF?

CARBON
18% carbon.
Many molecules in your body contain carbon! Carbon dioxide is expelled when you breathe out.

OXYGEN
65% oxygen.
It's in water, breathed in from air, and used to get energy from food.

HYDROGEN
10% hydrogen.
It's mostly in water. Like carbon, it's critical in chemical reactions.

NITROGEN
3% nitrogen.
It's very important for building proteins and in DNA.

CALCIUM
1.5% calcium.
It keeps your bones and teeth hard and strong.

PHOSPHORUS
1% phosphorus.
It's also found in bones, teeth, and energy molecules such as ATP.

YOU'RE ALSO
.4% potassium
.3% sulfur
.2% sodium
.2% chlorine
.05% magnesium
.006% iron
.004% iodine

PHOSPHORUS

A DEVILISH ELEMENT

FIERY AND TOXIC

PHOSPHORUS COMES IN WHITE, RED, VIOLET, OR BLACK.

Each kind, or allotrope, is toxic and super flammable. White phosphorus glows in the dark and just bursts into flame when it meets air! Yet our bodies need a little phosphorus to make DNA, and it's in the vital messenger chemical ATP. Bones and teeth are made from a phosphorus compound called calcium phosphate.

"THE DEVIL'S ELEMENT"

Phosphorus was discovered in urine in 1669. Urine is goldish in color. So German alchemist Hennig Brand thought it might contain the secret of the philosopher's stone, the magic substance that turns ordinary metal into gold. When Brand boiled urine down, he was left with a white powder that turned out to be a compound of phosphorus. The name for this glowing element is Greek for *bringer of light* and is the ancient name for the planet Venus when it appears before sunrise.

In World War II, Allied airplanes dropped terrible bombs of flaming phosphorus on the German city of Hamburg, and phosphorus is still used in weapons. Yet farmers apply phosphate (chemical compounds made from phosphorus) to soil to make crops grow better. And phosphorous is an ingredient in cola!

In the famous Sherlock Holmes detective story, *The Hound of the Baskervilles*, the awesome dog is painted with white phosphorus by the villains to make it glow in the dark and appear ultra-ghostly!

The first matches were tipped with white phosphorus to give an instant flame. This gave the women and girls who made them a horrible mouth condition called "phossy jaw." Today, safe, red phosphorus is used only in the strip you strike the match on.

PHOSPHORUS : At 68°F (20°C): Solid • Melting point (white): 111°F (44°C) • Boiling point (white): 536.5°F (280°C) • Color: None

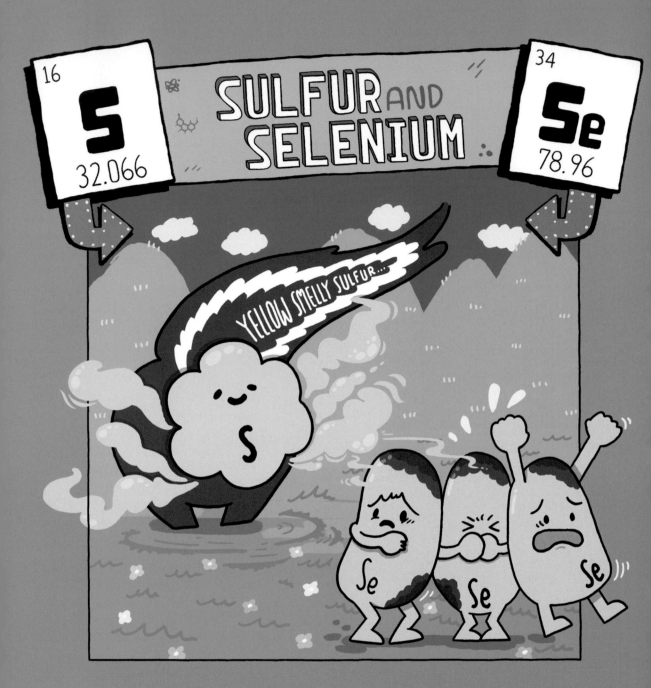

SULFUR and SELENIUM

16		34
S		**Se**
32.066		78.96

YELLOW SMELLY SULFUR...

STINKY!

SULFUR DOESN'T SMELL ITSELF, BUT ITS COMPOUNDS CAN STINK!

Sulfur oozes from volcanoes, on the land and the sea bed. It used to be called brimstone or "burning" stone because, like phosphorus, it bursts easily into flames. Fortunately, selenium isn't smelly. You can even find it in shampoo. But if you burn it, it smells of horseradish!

Don't get too close to a skunk. If you get splurged by skunk spray, you'll smell for days! That's because the spray is packed with smelly hydrogen sulfide compounds called thiols—the smells that make bad eggs and garlic stinky!

Sulfur's compound, hydrogen sulfide, puts the smell in farts! It smells so bad it can make people ill. That's why wastewater treatment plants have gas detectors! But sulfur isn't all smell. It's vital for your body, helping build proteins and bones.

In oxygen and heat, sulfur burns with a bright-blue flame. It's a key ingredient in gunpowder and still used in firecrackers! In 1844, Charles Goodyear accidentally discovered that heating Indian rubber and sulfur made the rubber ten times stronger. His process is now used to make all kinds of items from shoe soles to car tires.

SULFUR: At 68°F (20°C): Solid
Melting point: 239°F (115°C)
Boiling point: 833°F (445°C)
Color: Yellow

Selenium's a shape-shifter. Sometimes it comes as a silvery-gray solid that looks like metal, even though it's not. Sometimes it comes as a red powder, which is sometimes added to glass to make it a brilliant red.

Selenium is actually a vital component of your body. You need selenium in your food to keep your cells working properly. The highest levels are in your hair and liver. You can get a healthy amount of selenium by eating Brazil nuts, yellowfin tuna, whole-grain brown rice, liver, and kidney.

SELENIUM: At 68°F (20°C): Solid
Melting point: 430°F (221°C)
Boiling point: 1,265°F (685°C)
Color: Metallic gray

Water heated by hot or molten rocks inside Earth can burst through the crust in hot springs. It dissolves minerals on its journey, including those rich in selenium and sulfur, which can make the spring stinky!

FLUORINE AND CHLORINE ARE SUPER-REACTIVE AND VERY DANGEROUS. If fluorine gas hits anything—even glass—it instantly catches fire, and it just explodes when mixed with hydrogen. Exposure to air with just 0.1 percent of fluorine will kill you. Sadly, chlorine gas was used by Germany as a terrible weapon during World War I. And yet both these gases can be good for your health if used in the right way.

By itself, fluorine is a nasty, pale-yellow gas. But because each fluorine atom has a gap for a single electron in its outer shell, it teams up with just about any other atom and comes in many forms. It naturally occurs as a solid mineral called fluoride, for instance—and in tiny amounts fluoride is good for strong teeth, which is why it's put in toothpaste and sometimes in drinking water.

Teamed up with calcium, fluorine makes the mineral fluorite that not only comes in many colors but glows in the dark, which is how we got the word *fluorescent*.

FLUORINE: At 68°F (20°C): Gas
Melting point: -364°F (-220°C)
Boiling point: -307°F (-188°C)
Color: Pale yellow

Fluorine teamed with carbon makes fluorocarbons. One useful fluorocarbon is polytetrafluoroethylene or PTFE. But it's better known as Teflon (phew). It's the tough, nonstick coat on frying pans that helps with pancakes!

Fluorocarbons teamed with chlorine make chlorofluorocarbons (CFCs,) used for aerosols and in fridges to help keep them cool. But CFCs leak into the air and damage the ozone layer that protects us from dangerous rays from the sun. So they're banned now!

By itself, chlorine is a nasty, yellowy-green, poisonous gas. But you'll know the smell, because it's added to swimming pools to keep them free from germs and to bleach to keep toilets clean. Adding a little chlorine to water helps prevent diseases such as typhoid and cholera, and as a result it has saved millions of lives.

Like fluorine, chlorine is very reactive and forms thousands of compounds. The salt in your food and in the oceans is one of them—sodium chloride. Salt is so vital for health that Roman soldiers were given a regular salt allowance, giving us the word *salary*.

CHLORINE: At 68°F (20°C): Gas
Melting point: -151°F (-102°C)
Boiling point: -29°F (-34°C)
Color: Yellowy green

35 Br 79.904 BROMINE

Bromine is one of the stinkiest elements! At room temperature, it's a deep red liquid but it only has to get a little warm to start giving off smelly brown fumes. It's used as an alternative to chlorine sanitizer in hot tubs. It's great for putting out fires. But like CFCs, bromine damages the ozone layer in the atmosphere, so it's no longer widely used.

BROMINE: At 68°F (20°C): Liquid
Melting point: 19°F (-7.2°C)
Boiling point: 138°F (59°C)
Color: Deep red

53 I 126.90447 IODINE

Heat solid black iodine and it turns into a purple gas! Magic! It's quite rare, though there's plenty in the sea—and seaweed. Iodine in the thyroid gland in the neck helps produce the hormones that children need to grow. That's why iodine may be added to salt. Iodine was used to make the very first photographs in the 1830s. Fumes of bromine and iodine made the silver in exposed parts of the photo turn black to reveal the picture.

IODINE: At 68°F (20°C): Solid
Melting point: 237°F (114°C)
Boiling point: 364°F (184°C)
Color: Black with violet vapor

85 At 209.9871 ASTATINE

Astatine is super elusive and very, very rare. It's so rare that it's never been seen in pure form, which is why no one knows what color it is! It's a bit like iodine and vaporizes quickly. But it's also super radioactive, so it may be a good thing that it's so rare!

ASTATINE: At 68°F (20°C): Solid
Melting point: 576°F (302°C)
Boiling point: 639°F (337°C)
Color: Unknown

If you were a super-rich Roman, you'd wear a toga dyed in a deep color called Tyrian purple. Tyrian purple came from sea snails and got some of its color from bromine. It was rare and very, very expensive.

If you get a nasty cut or scrape, whoever is looking after you may dab iodine on the wound. It will sting a lot! But you don't have to worry. Iodine kills germs and it's been used to treat minor wounds for centuries. Without it, the wound might turn septic and full of puss!

Chemists have made one millionth of a gram of astatine altogether! But almost all of that has disintegrated. If chemists ever made enough to actually see, the intense heat of its radioactivity would make it vanish instantly. Chemists once thought it was the rarest element, but that's actually berkelium.

TOP GASES

WELCOME TO GROUP 18, ON THE EDGE

WHO MELTS FIRST?

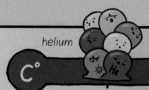 helium   −458°F (−272°C)

 neon   −415°F (−249°C)

argon   −308°F (−189°C)

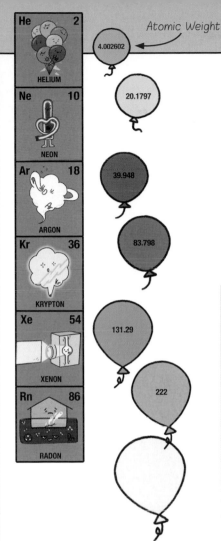

Atomic Weight

LONER GASES

This group is the very last column on the right of the table, and they're truly special. They're all colorless, odorless gases, and chemists call them "noble" gases. Their outer electron shell is full so they keep themselves to themselves. Some chemists call them "inert" because they just don't react. All the same, the heavier noble gases—krypton, xenon, and radon do occasionally form compounds.

INVISIBLE ELEMENTS

Because noble gases don't react, it was a long while before anyone realized they existed. But in the 1890s, the Scottish chemist, Sir William Ramsay, noticed that nitrogen in the lab was just a bit lighter than nitrogen in the air. He guessed there were other invisible gases making nitrogen in the air heavier. He soon discovered argon, then helium (known only in the sun until then), neon, krypton, and xenon. It meant the periodic table had to be entirely redrawn to add in Group 18.

If you want to keep things from getting out of hand, noble gases are for you because they don't react. In fact, we wouldn't have electric lights without noble gases. Electric light bulbs and tubes are filled with noble gases to stop the electric elements from burning out. Neon signs don't use just neon gas, but a mix of noble gases to make lights in brilliant colors.

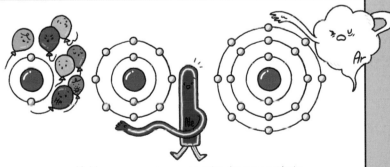

Noble gases are nonreactive because their outer electron shell is filled up.

krypton

xenon

radon

-243.8 (-153°C)   -169°F (-112°C)   -96°F (-71°C)

HELIUM

2
He
4.002602

SUPER LIGHT BALLOON FILLER

He

THE SECOND-OLDEST ELEMENT

HUH, YOU MAY THINK, THERE'S NOT MUCH TO HELIUM.

It's colorless, odorless, and barely reacts to anything. It's so light that if you let it go, it drifts up and up, into space and away. In fact, after hydrogen, helium is the lightest of all elements. But don't underestimate it! Helium is old. Very old. It's been around since the beginning of the universe and makes up over a quarter of the universe's mass.

PARTY TIME

No one knew helium existed until a French astronomer spotted unusual colors in the light coming from the sun in 1868. The colors revealed an unknown gas burning there. Scientists called this gas helium after *helios*, the Greek word for *sun*, and we now know it's one of the fuels that keeps stars burning.

It was soon found on Earth, too, in gases leaking from lava and in natural gas. It turned out to be very useful! Because it's so light, helium's great for filling party balloons! And when you need a gas that doesn't react, think of helium. Welders use it. And it saves deep-sea divers from getting too much oxygen from their oxygen supply. Meanwhile, your shopping in the grocery store is scanned by a helium neon laser. But we're running out of helium, because every time we use it, a little bit more of it drifts into space . . .

If you've got a party balloon filled with helium, ask an adult to help you with this trick. Untie the balloon carefully and breathe in the helium. Your voice goes cartoon squeaky! The sound vibrations from your voice travel faster in helium than air.

Cooled below -452°F (-269°C), helium becomes liquid, perfect for cooling the superconducting magnets used for MRI scans. Cooled a further two degrees, it becomes superweird helium (II) that can crawl out of jugs.

NOTHING BUT NOTHING MAKES NEON REACT . . .

except maybe fluorine. It's what scientists call an inert gas. Dull, huh? Oh no—when you electrify neon, it glows like nothing else! If you want a spectacular light show, neon's what you need. Neon's the gas that shines brilliant reds and oranges in the lights that make Times Square in New York and Las Vegas super glam.

NAME IN LIGHTS

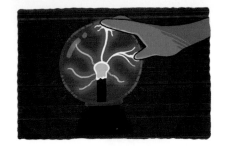

Neon is the fifth most abundant element in the universe, even though it is quite rare on Earth. Yet nobody knew about it until two British chemists went looking for it in 1898 to fill a gap in the periodic table. They collected a gas evaporating from argon and fired electrons at it in their spectrometer . . . *wham*! They saw a blaze of crimson. It was a glow like no one had ever seen.

That neon glow got everyone excited. Soon glitzy lights filled with neon gas were transforming city nights. Lots of colored lights are now called neon, but it's only red and orange that are true neon. Neon's now got many other uses, from TVs to aircraft landing lights.

In a plasma ball, neon is made to glow by streaming tendrils of high-voltage electricity emitted by an electrode in the middle. When you touch the outside, the tendril moves with you to change the pattern of light, because your body offers less electrical resistance than the glass.

Legend has it that the first neon signs in the USA were in Los Angeles in the 1920s. Carmakers Packard made a neon sign that so many people flocked to see, there were traffic jams!

NEON : At 68°F (20°C): Gas • Melting point: -415°F (-249°C) • Boiling point: -411°F (-246°C) • Color: None

Ar
18
39.948

ARGON

The name *argon* comes from the Greek for *lazy*, because it's a heavy gas that just doesn't react much. But it's the most abundant of the inert (unreactive) gases after helium, and it's put to work in many ways. Its idleness makes it perfect for adding to light bulbs to stop the elements from burning out. It's used in between glass panes in double glazing and in steelmaking to stop ingredients from oxidizing. It makes brilliant blue lights!

ARGON: At 68°F (20°C): Gas
Melting point: -309°F (-189°C)
Boiling point: -303°F (-186°C)
Color: None

Kr
36
83.798

KRYPTON

Krypton inspired the name for *kryptonite*, the substance that can weaken Superman! Kryptonite is a made-up green solid. Krypton is a real and colorless gas. All the same, it's hard to find—*krypton* is from the Greek word for *hidden*. Like argon, krypton is an inert gas useful for filling lights. It also makes brilliant blue-white strip lights and a deep violet laser beam. In 2007, Russian scientists found a mineral, jadarite, which matched all the qualities of the fictional kryptonite . . .

KRYPTON: At 68°F (20°C): Gas
Melting point: -243.8°F (-153°C)
Boiling point: -244°F (-153°C)
Color: None

54 Xe 131.29

XENON

Xenon is another gas that's really hard to pin down. The name *xenon* is from the Greek word for *stranger*. Like the other noble gases, it's colorless and inert, and forms compounds really rarely. Yet it may well become the fuel for the next generation of space probes. These will be powered by tiny ion engines. The ions are electrically charged atoms of xenon shot to propel the space probe at high speeds. Xenon also gives off a cool blue light in sunray lamps, photography, and car headlights.

XENON: At 68°F (20°C): Gas
Melting point: -169°F (-112°C)
Boiling point: -163°F (-108°C)
Color: None

86 Rn 222

RADON

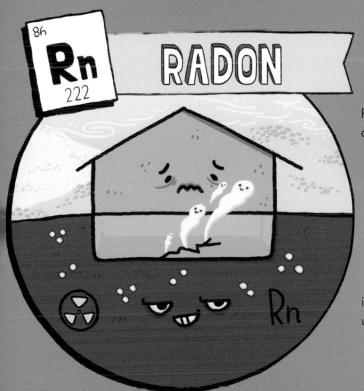

Radon is an inert, colorless gas like these others, but because its atoms are so big, they split up easily. So it's also highly radioactive. In fact, it could be one of the world's most dangerous gases. That's because it forms naturally through the radioactive decay of uranium and thorium in granite rock. Because it's so heavy, it can collect in the basement of buildings made of granite, or in valleys in granite regions. The doses of radon are usually too low to harm anyone.

RADON: Phase: Gas
Melting point: -96°F (-71°C)
Boiling point: -79°F (-62°C)
Color: None

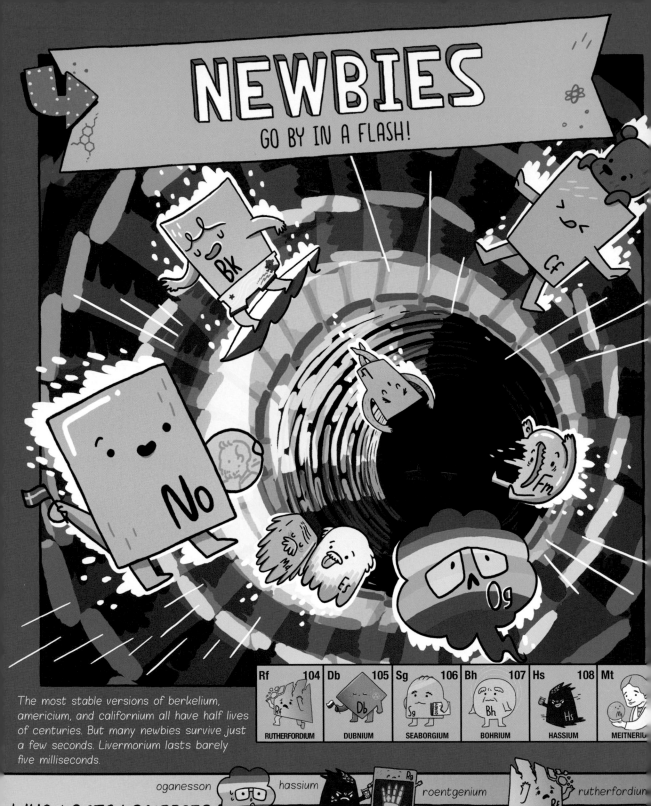

NEWBIES
GO BY IN A FLASH!

The most stable versions of berkelium, americium, and californium all have half lives of centuries. But many newbies survive just a few seconds. Livermorium lasts barely five milliseconds.

Rf 104	Db 105	Sg 106	Bh 107	Hs 108	Mt
RUTHERFORDIUM	DUBNIUM	SEABORGIUM	BOHRIUM	HASSIUM	MEITNERIUM

WHO LASTS LONGEST?

oganesson	hassium	roentgenium	rutherfordium
0.0009 seconds	22 seconds	26 seconds	1.3 hours

MAKING ELEMENTS

The first 94 elements in the periodic table, to plutonium, were forged naturally in the stars. But over the last 70 years, scientists have forged new atoms themselves to add to the table. They've made more than 20 of these synthetic elements so far. More are surely on the way.

How do you make an element? You smash atoms together until they combine into new, heavier elements. To make livermorium, scientists hurled atoms of calcium at curium. To make oganesson, they hurled calcium at californium. It's exceptionally hard to do. You can do it in nuclear reactors, in explosions, or you can do it in a more controlled way in a particle accelerator.

Synthetic elements have no staying power at all! They all start breaking up as soon as they're made. Scientists measure their lifetime in terms of half-life, which is the time it takes for half of their atoms to break up.

The odd one out! Newbies are usually scientists' one-offs. But curium's made again and again in nuclear reactors, and traces may occur naturally in uranium.

Am 95	Cm 96	Bk 97	Cf 98	Es 99	Fm 100	Md 101	No 102	Lr 103
AMERICIUM	CURIUM	BERKELIUM	CALIFORNIUM	EINSTEINIUM	FERMIUM	MENDELEVIUM	NOBELIUM	LAWRENCIUM

110	Rg 111	Cn 112	Nh 113	Fl 114	Mc 115	Lv 116	Ts 117	Og 118
DARMSTADTIUM	ROENTGENIUM	COPERNICIUM	NIHONIUM	FLEROVIUM	MOSCOVIUM	LIVERMORIUM	TENNESSINE	OGANESSON

 einsteinium   *californium*   *americium*

129 years   900 years   7470 years

ACTINOID NEWBIES

AMERICIUM

95 Am 243

When American scientists first made americium in World War II they kept it secret, just in case it had military uses. But now, there's a tiny amount inside many smoke detectors.

AMERICIUM:
At 68°F (20°C): Solid
Melting point: 2,149°F (1,176°C)
Boiling point: 3,652°F (2,011°C)
Color: Silver

BERKELIUM

97 Bk 247

Berkelium is named after the University of California, Berkeley (UC Berkeley), where it was made in 1949. It's the rarest element on Earth, but is used to make heavier elements such as tennessine.

BERKELIUM:
At 68°F (20°C): Solid
Melting point: 1,922°F (1,050°C)
Boiling point: 4,760.6°F (2,627°C)
Color: Unknown

CALIFORNIUM

98 Cf 251

Californium was first made at UC Berkeley in 1950. Its strong, radioactive rays are great for scanning baggage for explosives, and for huntin for gold and oil. Californium is also used for making medical MRI scans clearer.

CALIFORNIUM:
At 68°F (20°C): Solid
Melting point: 1,652°F (900°C)
Boiling point: Unknown
Color: Unknown

EINSTEINIUM

99 Es 252

Einsteinium was discovered in the fallout from a nuclear bomb test on Eniwetok atoll in the Pacific in 1952. It was named after Albert Einstein whose work explained how energy could be released in an atomic bomb, though he hated atomic weapons.

EINSTEINIUM:
At 68°F (20°C): Solid
Melting point: 1,580°F (860°C)
Boiling point: 1,824.8°F (996°C)
Color: Unknown

FERMIUM

100 Fm 257

Once, long ago, fermium existed on Earth. But it was only found, like einsteinium, in the fallout from the Eniwetok nuclear test. If it could be made to last more than a few months, it might be used to treat cancer.

FERMIUM:
At 68°F (20°C): Solid
Melting point: 2,781°F (1,527°C)
Boiling point: Unknown
Color: Unknown

101 Md MENDELEVIUM
258

Mendelevium was first made from einsteinium in UC Berkeley's "cyclotron," a particle machine. But so few atoms have ever been created that no one has actually seen it.

MENDELEVIUM:
At 68°F (20°C): Solid
Melting point: 827°C (1521°F)
Boiling point: Unknown
Color: Unknown

102 No NOBELIUM
259.1

From the 1950s, American, Russian, and Swedish scientists argued that they had created element 102. It was named for Alfred Nobel, who launched the Nobel Prizes.

NOBELIUM:
At 68°F (20°C): Solid
Melting point: 1,520°F (827°C)
Boiling point: Unknown
Color: Unknown

103 Lr LAWRENCIUM
262

American and Russian scientists competed to make element 103. The Americans possibly won, and it was named after Ernest Lawrence who invented the cyclotron in 1929 and was awarded a Nobel Prize in Physics.

LAWRENCIUM:
At 68°F (20°C): Solid
Melting point: 2,961°F (1,627°C)
Boiling point: Unknown
Color: Unknown

117 Ts TENNESSINE
294

The second-heaviest known atom, tennessine, was made by Russian and American scientists together in 2010. They named it after the state of Tennessee, and put "ine" in the name because it's probably a halogen like fluorine and chlorine.

TENNESSINE:
At 68°F (20°C): Solid
Melting point: Unknown
Boiling point: Unknown
Color: Unknown

118 Og OGANESSON
294

The heaviest atom of all, oganesson was first made by a team led by Russian scientist Yuri Oganessian in 2002 by bombarding californium atoms with calcium. It's probably a noble gas like radon.

OGANESSON:
At 68°F (20°C): Gas
Melting point: Unknown
Boiling point: unknown
Color: Unknown

SHE DISCOVERED IT!

For more than a century, women scientists have played a critical role in the teams discovering new elements and more about atoms:

IDA NODDACK (1896–1978) rhenium
MARIE CURIE (1867–1934) polonium, radium, and all about radioactivity
IRÉNE JOLIOT-CURIE (1897–1956) artificial radioactivity
BERTA KARLIK (1904–1990) astatine
MARGUERITE PEREY (1909–1975) francium
LISE MEITNER (1878–1968) nuclear fission (how atoms split) and protactinium
CLARICE PHELPS, tennessine, currently studying isotopes for industrial use

TOUGH METAL NEWBIES

104
Rf
267

RUTHERFORDIUM:
At 68°F (20°C): Solid
Melting point: Unknown
Boiling point: Unknown
Color: Probably silver

Rutherfordium is probably a silvery metal that corrodes in the air, but who knows? It doesn't hang around long enough for anyone to tell! It was created by bombarding californium with calcium in the 1960s.

105
Db
268

DUBNIUM:
At 68°F (20°C): Solid
Melting point: Unknown
Boiling point: Unknown
Color: Probably silver

Super-heavy, radioactive dubnium is named after Dubna in Russia where it was first made at the JINR research lab. Various names were tried out including nielsbohrium and hahnium before it was agreed to name it dubnium.

106
Sg
269

SEABORGIUM:
At 68°F (20°C): Unknown
Melting point: Unknown
Boiling point: Unknown
Color: Probably silver

Seaborgium is probably a radioactive metal. It was discovered at UC Berkeley in tiny amounts, spotted after a while by bombarding californium atoms with oxygen. It is named after American chemist Glenn Seaborg, co-discoverer of 10 elements.

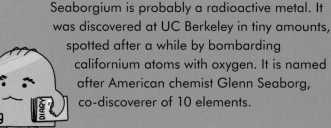

107
Bh
270

BOHRIUM:
At 68°F (20°C): Solid
Melting point: Unknown
Boiling point: Unknown
Color: Probably silver

Bohrium was first made in Dubna in Russia in 1975 by smashing bismuth and chromium atoms together. It's named after Danish scientist Niels Bohr who proposed the idea of electron shells.

HASSIUM

| 108 |
| Hs |
| 269 |

HASSIUM:
At 68°F (20°C): Solid
Melting point: Unknown
Boiling point: Unknown
Color: Probably silver

Hassium could be osmium's twin, except that it's highly radioactive. It was first made both in Dubna, Russia, and Darmstadt, Germany; Darmstadt's in the state of Hesse—so it was named hassium.

MEITNERIUM

| 109 |
| Mt |
| 278 |

MEITNERIUM:
At 68°F (20°C): Unknown
Melting point: Unknown
Boiling point: Unknown
Color: Unknown

Meitnerium could be iridium's twin, just a bit heavier. It's named after Austrian physicist Lise Meitner, who pioneered nuclear fission (splitting atomic nuclei to release their energy).

DARMSTADTIUM

| 110 |
| Ds |
| 281 |

DARMSTADTIUM:
At 68°F (20°C): Solid
Melting point: Unknown
Boiling point: Unknown
Color: Unknown

Super heavy and highly radioactive, darmstadtium should be a noble metal. No, not metal royalty like gold—just unreactive, like the noble gases neon and argon. It was first made in Darmstadt, Germany, in 1994. Some suggested calling it politzium since 110 is the emergency number for the *polizei* (police) in Germany.

ROENTGENIUM

| 111 |
| Rg |
| 280 |

ROENTGENIUM:
At 68°F (20°C): Solid
Melting point: Unknown
Boiling point: Unknown
Color: Unknown

First made in Darmstadt and Dubna, roentgenium is probably a noble metal and resists corrosion and oxidation. It's super heavy, super rare, and only a few atoms of it ever form.

COPERNICIUM

| 112 |
| Cn |
| 285 |

COPERNICIUM:
At 68°F (20°C): Solid
Melting point: Unknown
Boiling point: Unknown
Color: Unknown

Named after 16th-century astronomer Nicolaus Copernicus. Scientists at Darmstadt, Germany, hurled zinc ions into lead at 67 million mph (108 million kph) for two weeks to make it.

113 Nh 286 NIHONIUM

Only a few atoms of nihonium have ever been made and they decay in seconds. The Japanese team who won the official credit for making it named it after Nihon, a common name for Japan.

NIHONIUM:
Phase: At 68°F (20°C): Solid
Melting point: Unknown
Boiling point: Unknown
Color: Unknown

114 Fl 289 FLEROVIUM

To make one atom of flerovium, a Russian team fired five billion billion atoms of calcium at plutonium. It's hard to tell, but it seems to behave like both a metal and a noble gas. So, along with copernicium, it's called a "volatile metal."

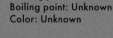

FLEROVIUM:
At 68°F (20°C): Solid
Melting point: Unknown
Boiling point: Unknown
Color: Unknown

115 Mc 288 MOSCOVIUM

Only a few atoms of moscovium have been made, at Dubna in Russia—so it's named after . . . Moscow, Russia's capital. It's likely to be a solid metal that quickly decays into other elements, such as nihonium.

MOSCOVIUM :
At 68°F (20°C): Solid
Melting point: Unknown
Boiling point: Unknown
Color: Unknown

116 Lv 293 LIVERMORIUM

Livermorium was first made in Russia by bombarding curium with calcium. But the Russian scientists named it after the Lawrence Livermore National Laboratory in the US, which supplied the curium. It's so hard to make, very little is known about it.

LIVERMORIUM:
At 68°F (20°C): Solid
Melting point: Unknown
Boiling point: Unknown
Color: Unknown

GLOSSARY

ACID A chemical that is usually corrosive. Acids turn indicator paper or litmus paper a red color.

ALKALI A chemical that dissolves in water. An alkali is the chemical opposite of an acid and turns litmus paper blue.

ALLOTROPE One of two or more distinct forms of the same element that have different properties but are the same state of matter (solid, liquid, or gas). Diamond is an allotrope of carbon.

ALLOY A mixture of metals, or a mixture of a metal with a nonmetal element.

ATOM The basic part of an element. Atoms are made up of smaller particles: protons, neutrons, and electrons.

ATOMIC NUMBER The number of protons in the nucleus of an atom.

CATALYST A substance that increases the rate of a chemical reaction without itself undergoing any lasting change.

CATALYTIC CONVERTER A control device for engines, such as car engines, in which elements act as catalysts, to change exhaust gases from polluting ones to less polluting ones in reactions.

COMBUSTION A reaction in which a substance reacts with oxygen in the air and transfers energy to its surroundings in the form of light and heat.

COMPOUND A substance made of two or more elements that are combined, or linked together, chemically.

CONDUCTIVITY The ability or power of a material that allows heat or electricity to pass through it.

CORROSION The chemical breakdown of the surface of a metal.

CRYSTAL A solid with a regular microscopic framework of atoms, ions, or molecules, such as in metals. Or it can be a mineral with a geometric shape.

ELECTRON A negatively charged particle that orbits the nucleus of an atom.

ELECTROMAGNET A coil of wire which becomes magnetic when an electric current flows through the coil.

ELEMENT A substance which is made of only one type of atom.

FISSION The splitting of a heavy atomic nuclei to form two lighter ones. Energy is released in the process.

FLUORESCENCE Colored light given off by certain substances after exposure to ultraviolet light.

FUSION The combining of very light atomic nuclei to form a heavier nucleus. Energy is released in the process.

GAS A state of matter in which atoms are free to move around, enabling the substance to fill a container.

HALF-LIFE The time it takes for half of the atoms in a radioactive element to decay.

HYDROCARBON A compound burned in the presence of oxygen to produce light, carbon dioxide, water, and heat.

INERT Unlikely or unable to react chemically.

INFRARED Invisibly long waves of electromagnetic radiation that can be felt as heat.

ION An atom that has either lost or gained at least one electron so that it is positively or negatively charged.

ISOTOPE Different versions of the atoms of one element. They have the same number of electrons and protons but different numbers of neutrons.

LASER An intense beam of light used for surgery, measurement, and more.

LIQUID A state of matter between solid and gas. A liquid can flow, and it will always take the shape of its container.

MAGNET A substance or object that attracts iron, cobalt, nickel, gadolinium, and their alloys.

METEORITE A fragment of rock from outer space that reaches Earth's surface instead of completely burning up in the atmosphere.

MINERAL A natural solid with a distinct chemical composition and often made of crystals. Nearly all rocks are made of minerals.

MIXTURE In chemistry, a mixture contains different substances that are not chemically joined to each other.

MOLECULE The smallest identifiable group of atoms for a particular element or compound.

MRI SCANNER A machine that provides detailed images of sections of the human body that are used for medical diagnosis. MRI stands for Magnetic Resonance Imaging.

NEUTRON A particle in the atom's nucleus that has no electrical charge, slightly bigger than a proton.

NUCLEAR Relating to the nucleus, or core of an atom.

NUCLEAR REACTOR The structure that contains and controls the nuclear reaction produced through fission, releasing energy.

NUCLEUS The positively charged central area of an atom, composed of neutrons, protons, and almost all of the mass.

ORE A metal-bearing mineral or rock that can be mined.

OXIDATION When a substance gains oxygen.

OZONE A colorless gas that is an unstable, poisonous allotrope of oxygen.

PARTICLE ACCELERATOR A machine that uses magnets to accelerate subatomic particles around a track. Collisions between the particles releases energy and might create new particles or elements.

PROTON A positively charged particle found in the nucleus of an atom.

RADIATION Anything that radiates from its source. It could be waves, such as light or sound, or it could be a beam of invisible particles, such as neutrons.

RADIOACTIVE DECAY The natural breakup of atomic nuclei in radioactive elements.

RADIOACTIVITY The emission of nuclear radiation.

REACTIVE Describes an element or compound that reacts and changes when it meets other chemicals.

SEMICONDUCTOR A material whose electrical conductivity varies between that of a metal and a nonmetal. Semiconductors are often made of metalloid compounds.

SOLID A state of matter in which the particles are packed tightly together so they are unable to move around very much.

SUPERNOVA A huge explosion that takes place when a giant star has used up all of its fuel.

SYNTHETIC Describes an element that is created artificially, often inside nuclear reactors and particle accelerators.

UV OR ULTRAVIOLET RADIATION Invisible electromagnetic waves with wavelengths that are shorter than wavelengths of visible light and longer than those of X-rays.

X-RAY A high frequency wave of electromagnetic energy that is absorbed by body tissues and used in medicine to produce images inside the human body.

INDEX

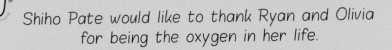

Shiho Pate would like to thank Ryan and Olivia
for being the oxygen in her life.

And all the scientists and future scientists out there.

Illustrated by Shiho Pate
Written by John Farndon
Consultant editor: Lesley-Ann Giddings, Assistant Professor of Chemistry, Smith College
Art Director: Zoë Tucker

Library of Congress Cataloging-in-Publication Data available

ISBN 978-1-338-75365-3

10 9 8 7 6 5 4 3 2   21 22 23 24 25

Printed in China   38
First edition, October 2021

1

H

1.00794

Oh wow! Hydrogen is the only element in the universe with no neutrons at all!

HYDROGEN

Family: **Alkali metals**
At 68°F (20°C): **Gas** • Color: **None**
Melting point: **−434°F (−259°C)**
Boiling point: **−423°F (−253°C)**

2

He

4.002602

Oh wow! Helium is so light that Earth's gravity just can't hold on to it.

HELIUM

Family: **Noble gases**
At 68°F (20°C): **Gas** • Color: **None**
Melting point: **−458°F (−272°C)**
Boiling point: **−452°F (−269°C)**

3

Li

6.941

Oh wow! The lightest metal, is found in the rechargeable battery of your phone, laptop, or camera.

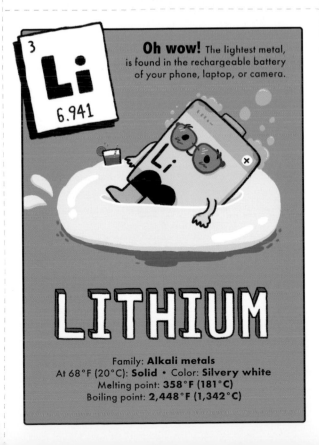

LITHIUM

Family: **Alkali metals**
At 68°F (20°C): **Solid** • Color: **Silvery white**
Melting point: **358°F (181°C)**
Boiling point: **2,448°F (1,342°C)**

6

C

12.0107

Oh wow! You can't melt a diamond! It never turns liquid—it turns straight to vapor!

CARBON

Family: **Nonmetals**
At 68°F (20°C): **Solid** • Color: **Silvery white**
Melting point: **6,422°F (3,550°C)**
Boiling point: **6,917°F (3,825°C)**

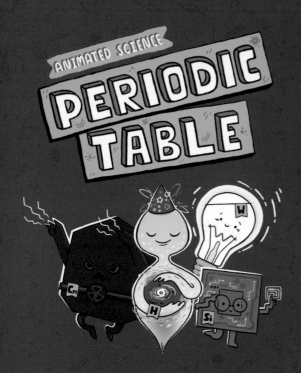

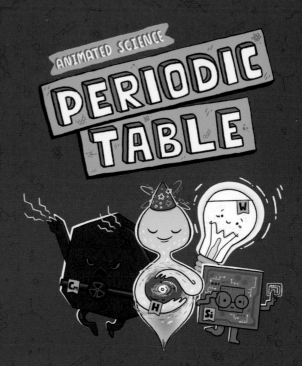

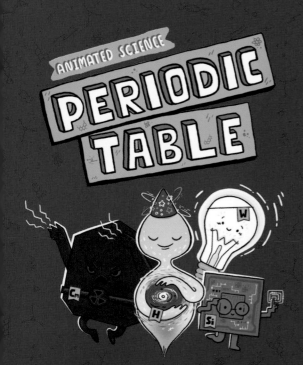

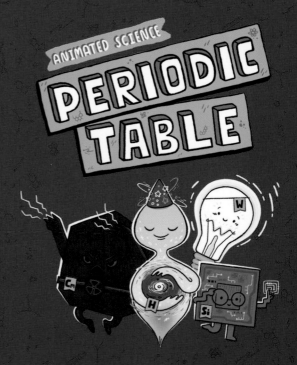

ALUMINUM

13
Al
26.982

Oh wow! Aluminum used to be so hard to obtain that they called it the "Metal of Kings."

Family: **Poor metals**
At 68°F (20°C): **Solid** • Color: **Silvery white**
Melting point: **1,220.58°F (660.32°C)**
Boiling point: **4,478°F (2,470°C)**

SILICON

14
Si
28.0855

Oh wow! In 2017, scientists created the first 5-nanometer silicon computer chip.

Family: **Metalloids**
At 68°F (20°C): **Solid** • Color: **Bluish, metallic**
Melting point: **2,577°F (1,414°C)**
Boiling point: **5,909°F (3,265°C)**

SULFUR

16
S
32.066

Oh wow! The world's first explosive gunpowder was made from stinky sulfur. *Bang!*

Family: **Nonmetals**
At 68°F (20°C): **Solid** • Color: **Yellow**
Melting point: **239°F (115°C)**
Boiling point: **833°F (445°C)**

POTASSIUM

19
K
39.0983

Oh wow! To stay healthy, eat bananas and fresh veggies. They don't look metallic, but they're rich in potassium!

Family: **Alkali metals**
At 68°F (20°C): **Solid** • Color: **Silvery white**
Melting point: **146.3°F (63.5°C)**
Boiling point: **1,398°F (759°C)**

ANIMATED SCIENCE

PERIODIC TABLE

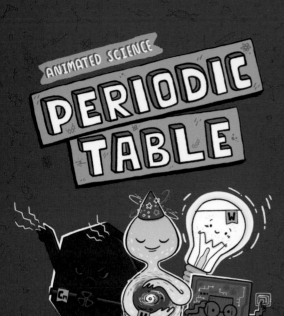

ANIMATED SCIENCE

PERIODIC TABLE

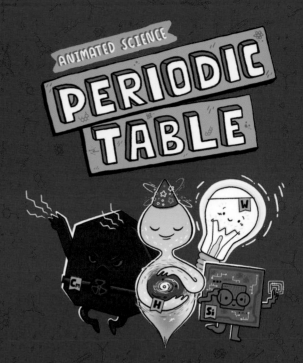

ANIMATED SCIENCE

PERIODIC TABLE

ANIMATED SCIENCE

PERIODIC TABLE

Ti

22

Ti

47.867

Oh wow! If you want titanium, go to the moon. There are rocks there that are 10 percent titanium!

TITANIUM

Family: **Transition metals**
At 68°F (20°C): **Solid** • Color: **Silver**
Melting point: **3,034°F (1,668°C)**
Boiling point: **5,949°F (3,287°C)**

Fe

26

Fe

55.845

Oh wow! Iron is the end of the road for giant stars. When a star's core turns to iron, it's soon going to explode or collapse into a black hole!

IRON

Family: **Transition metals**
At 68°F (20°C): **Solid** • Color: **Silvery gray**
Melting point: **2,800°F (1,538°C)**
Boiling point: **5,182°F (2,861°C)**

Cu

29

Cu

63.546

Oh wow! Otzi the Iceman was found frozen in the Alps 5,300 years after he died. His axe was made of almost pure copper!

COPPER

Family: **Transition metals**
At 68°F (20°C): **Solid** • Color: **Reddish orange**
Melting point: **1,984°F (1,084°C)**
Boiling point: **4,644°F (2,562°C)**

Au

79

Au

196.96655

Oh wow! Turning ordinary metals into gold was the never-achieved goal of medieval alchemists. But modern nuclear scientists can do it.

GOLD

Family: **Transition metals**
At 68°F (20°C): **Solid** • Color: **Metallic yellow**
Melting point: **1,947.5°F (1,064°C)**
Boiling point: **5,172.8°F (2,856°C)**

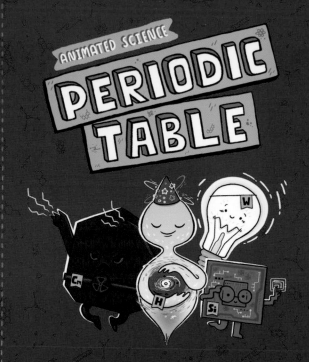

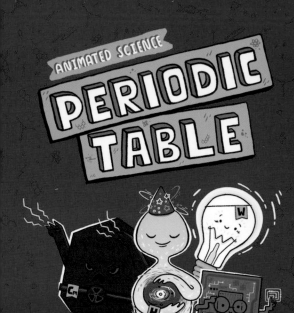

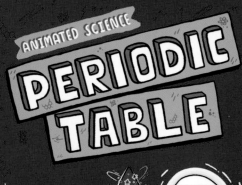

80 · Hg · 200.592

Oh wow! At the 1937 International Exhibition in Paris, a fountain was made of mercury. You can still see it gushing today at the *Fundació Joan Miró* in Barcelona, Spain.

MERCURY

Family: **Transition metals**
At 68°F (20°C): **Liquid** • Color: **Silver**
Melting point: **−38°F (−39°C)**
Boiling point: **674.1°F (357°C)**

85 · At · 209.9871

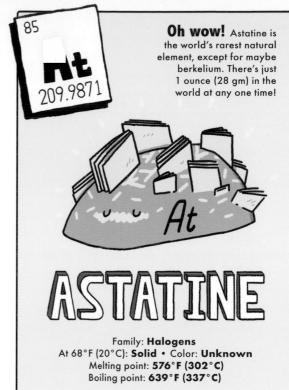

Oh wow! Astatine is the world's rarest natural element, except for maybe berkelium. There's just 1 ounce (28 gm) in the world at any one time!

ASTATINE

Family: **Halogens**
At 68°F (20°C): **Solid** • Color: **Unknown**
Melting point: **576°F (302°C)**
Boiling point: **639°F (337°C)**

92 · U · 238.02891

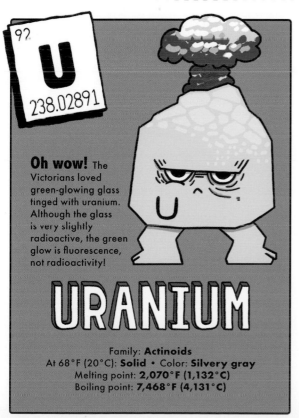

Oh wow! The Victorians loved green-glowing glass tinged with uranium. Although the glass is very slightly radioactive, the green glow is fluorescence, not radioactivity!

URANIUM

Family: **Actinoids**
At 68°F (20°C): **Solid** • Color: **Silvery gray**
Melting point: **2,070°F (1,132°C)**
Boiling point: **7,468°F (4,131°C)**

118 · Og · 294

Oh wow! No one is quite sure whether oganesson will be a solid or the densest gas ever.

OGANESSON

Family: **Noble gases**
At 68°F (20°C): **Gas** • Color: **Unknown**
Melting point: **Unknown**
Boiling point: **Unknown**

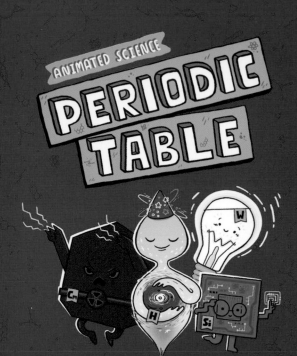

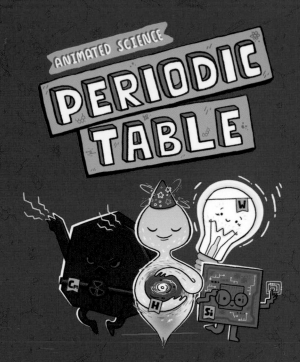

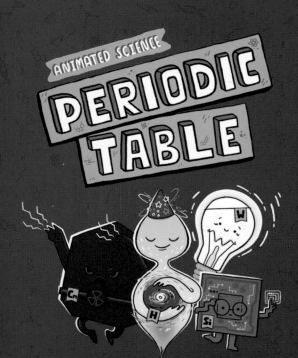

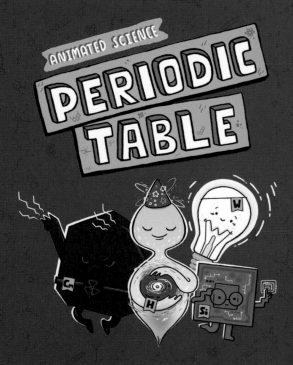